Copyright © 2011 Concordia Publishing House
3558 S. Jefferson Avenue, St. Louis, MO 63118-3968
1-800-325-3040 • www.cph.org

Manufactured in the United States of America

1 2 3 4 5 6 7 8 9 10   20 19 18 17 16 15 14 13 12 11

LUTHER

THE GRAPHIC NOVEL

By Susan K. Leigh

❖

Illustrated by
Dave Hill

Echoes of the Hammer

CONCORDIA PUBLISHING HOUSE · SAINT LOUIS

Castle Church
✦ Wittenberg

Birth House
✦ Eisleben

Wartburg Castle
✦ Eisenach

Augustinerklost
✦ Erfurt

Worms
Cathedral

Augsburg
Confession

This is the story of
Martin Luther,
a hero of the church.

The reformer Martin Luther was an influential man who launched widespread change in the Christian Church and consequently laid a new foundation for society. But what he wanted more than anything was peace with God.

As a young monk, Luther searched the Bible to ease his anxieties about sin and salvation. As he studied the Scriptures, he became convinced that the Roman Catholic Church had lost sight of its central teachings. He challenged the church to return to the roots of the Christian faith by posting his Ninety-five Theses on the door of the Castle Church in Wittenberg, an act that guaranteed attention.

The church leaders liked things the way they were, however, and tried to stop Martin Luther. But despite its best efforts, the hierarchy of the church could not suppress him. Luther stood his ground, and his tireless work led to the reformation of the church and to far-reaching changes in society.

Here is the story of adventure, courage, and faith. Here is the story of a hero of the church.

"Grant that I may not pray alone with the mouth; help me that I may pray from the depths of my heart."

❖ Luther's Early Years

Eisleben, Germany—1483

Another son, Margaret! Praise God for your health and his!

The next day, Hans Luther takes his new son to the Church of Saints Peter and Paul to be baptized.

The day is November 11, the festival of St. Martin of Tours. As was the custom, children were named for the saint day they were born on.

I baptize you in the name of the Father, and of the Son, and of the Holy Ghost.

St. Martin of Tours was a fourth-century Christian who traveled throughout Europe to spread the Gospel. November 11 is observed as the day of his burial. The historical Feast of St. Martin lasted 40 days and is the forerunner to the season of Advent.

The Luther family moves to Mansfeld, where Hans works in a copper mine.

Hans prospers in his work, buys his own mines and smelting furnaces, and is eventually elected to the city council.

Like other German Catholic families in Mansfeld, the Luthers attend Mass at St. George's Church. The priest chants the Mass in Latin, which would have confused young Martin, who knew only German.

Because they didn't know otherwise, and because the Bible was not available to them in their own language to read,

people viewed God as a harsh judge.

They believed that Jesus was distant and unavailable to them. Paintings of Jesus frightened young Martin.

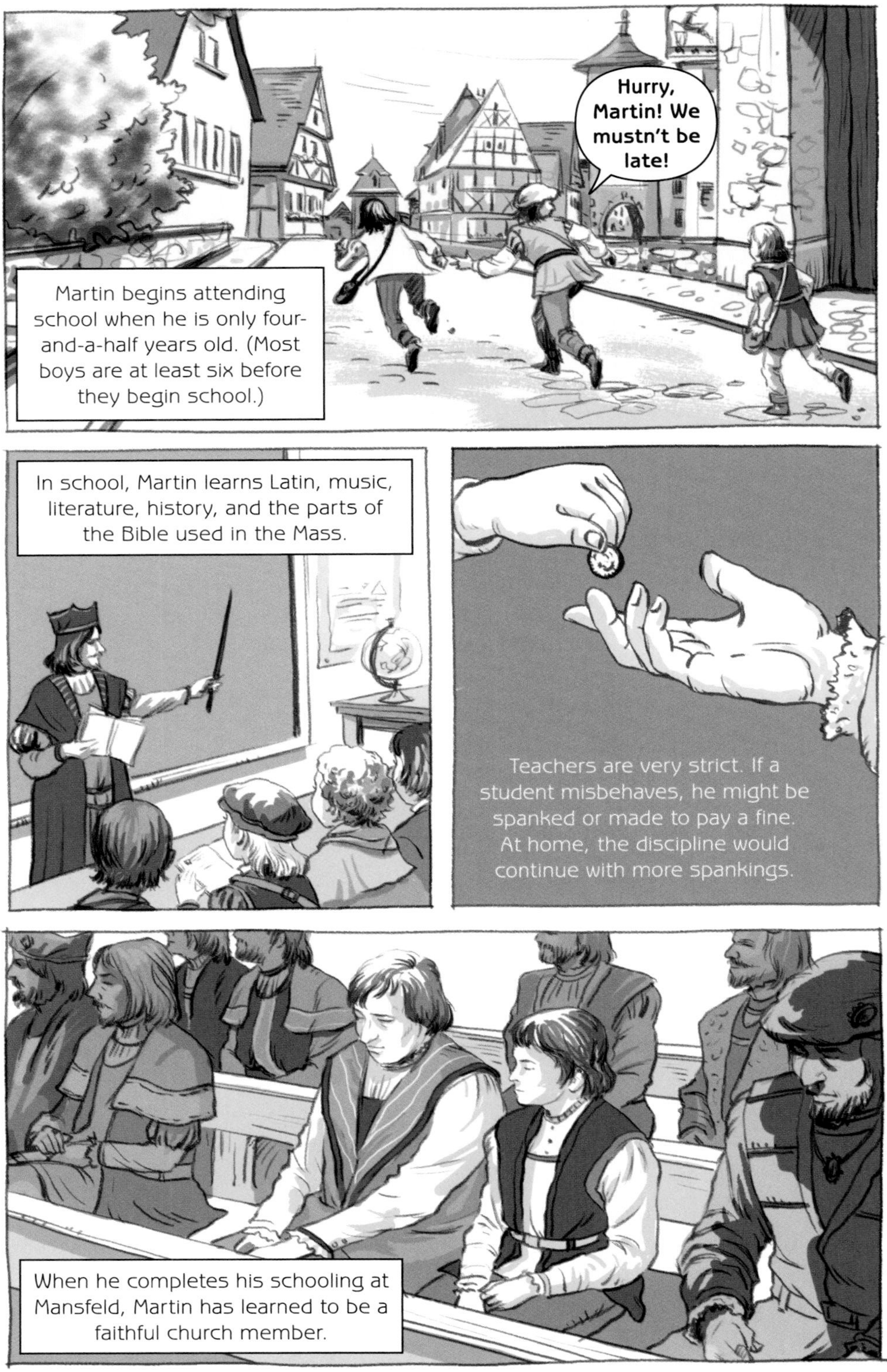
Martin begins attending school when he is only four-and-a-half years old. (Most boys are at least six before they begin school.)
Hurry, Martin! We mustn't be late!
In school, Martin learns Latin, music, literature, history, and the parts of the Bible used in the Mass.
Teachers are very strict. If a student misbehaves, he might be spanked or made to pay a fine. At home, the discipline would continue with more spankings.
When he completes his schooling at Mansfeld, Martin has learned to be a faithful church member.

When he is 14, Martin goes to Magdeburg, 60 miles from home, to attend the highly respected cathedral schools.

Look at the spires of the cathedral, Martin! Have you ever seen such a sight?

Martin and his friend John Reinecke, along with other students, beg for coins on the city streets. This is a common practice and people willingly give small coins to the boys.

Singing for your supper, boys? Here's a coin for your effort!

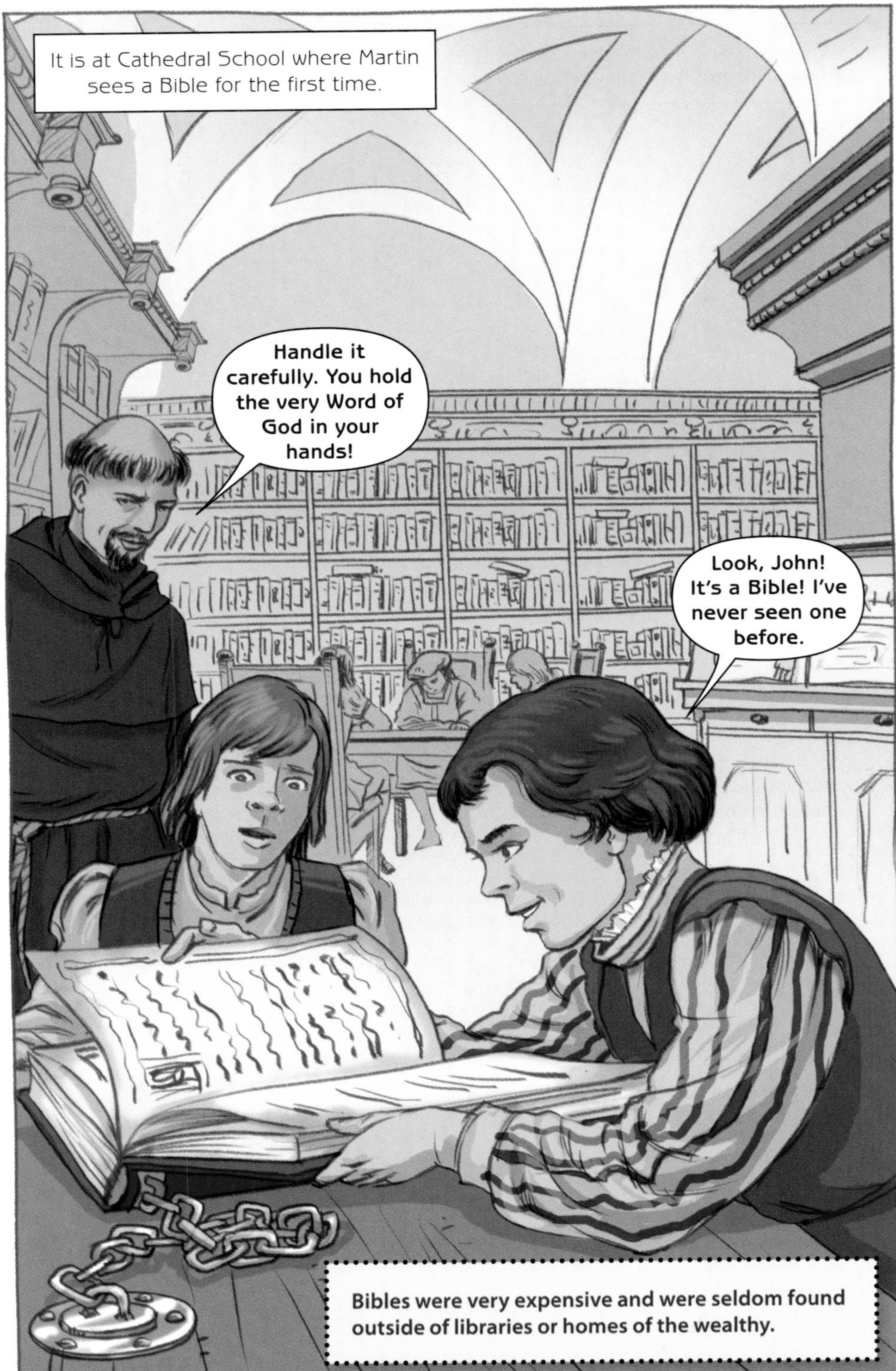
It is at Cathedral School where Martin sees a Bible for the first time.
Handle it carefully. You hold the very Word of God in your hands!
Look, John! It's a Bible! I've never seen one before.
Bibles were very expensive and were seldom found outside of libraries or homes of the wealthy.

A year later, Martin transfers to the Latin school of St. George's Church in Eisenach to prepare for university. These were among the happiest years of his young life.

The Lord has blessed you, Martin. You must use His gifts faithfully and in His service.

In May 1501, Martin enrolls at the university in Erfurt—the best university in all of Germany. He graduates in September 1502, at 18, with a bachelor of arts degree. Then, in 1505, he earns a master of arts degree, also from Erfurt.

I'm proud of you, son. You will continue your studies. And one day, you will be a fine lawyer.

With his father's blessing, Martin stays at Erfurt to study law.

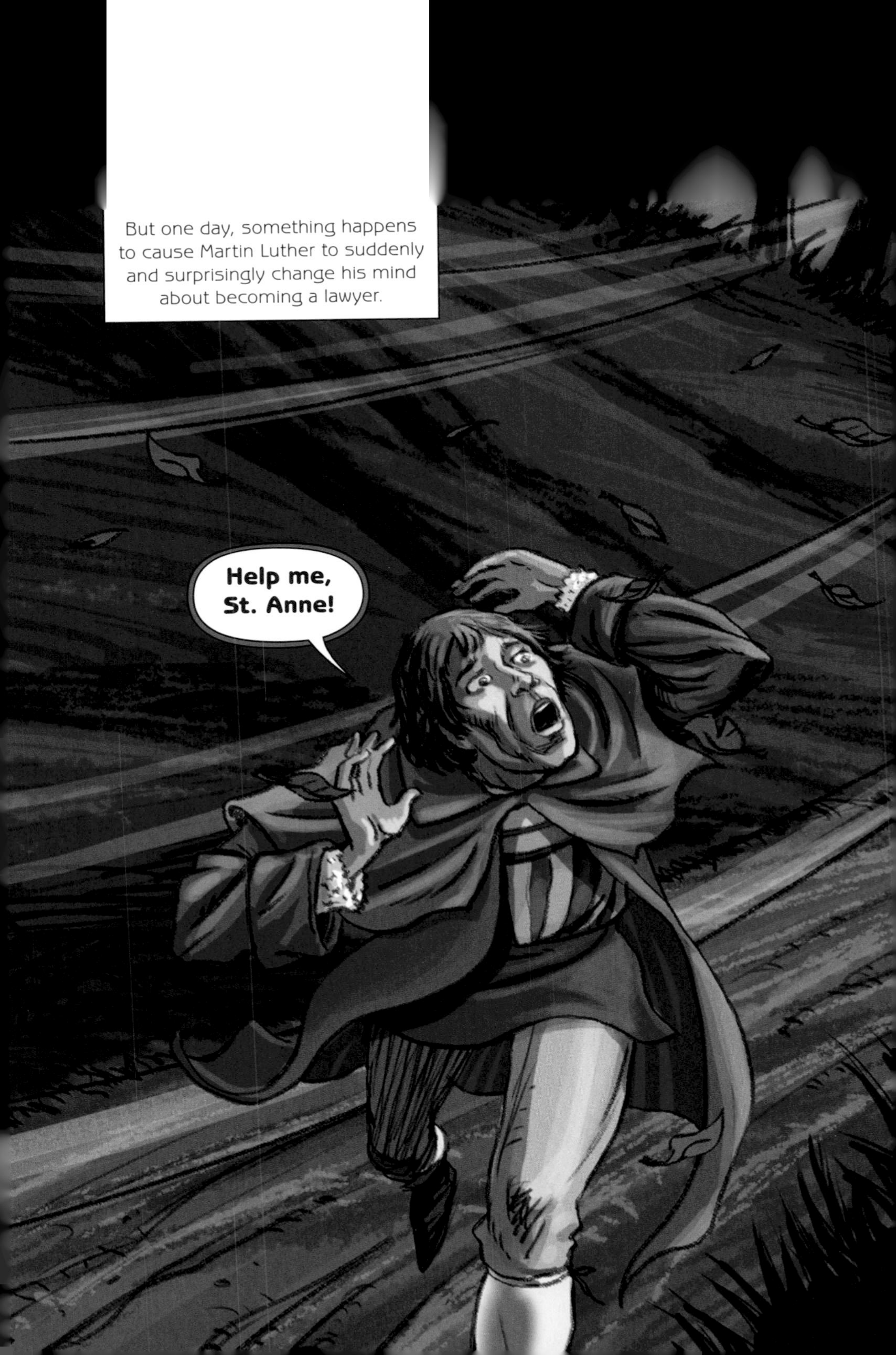
But one day, something happens to cause Martin Luther to suddenly and surprisingly change his mind about becoming a lawyer.
Help me, St. Anne!

As he walked back to Erfurt after a visit with his family, a sudden storm frightened him. He vowed that if he were to live through the storm, he would become a monk.

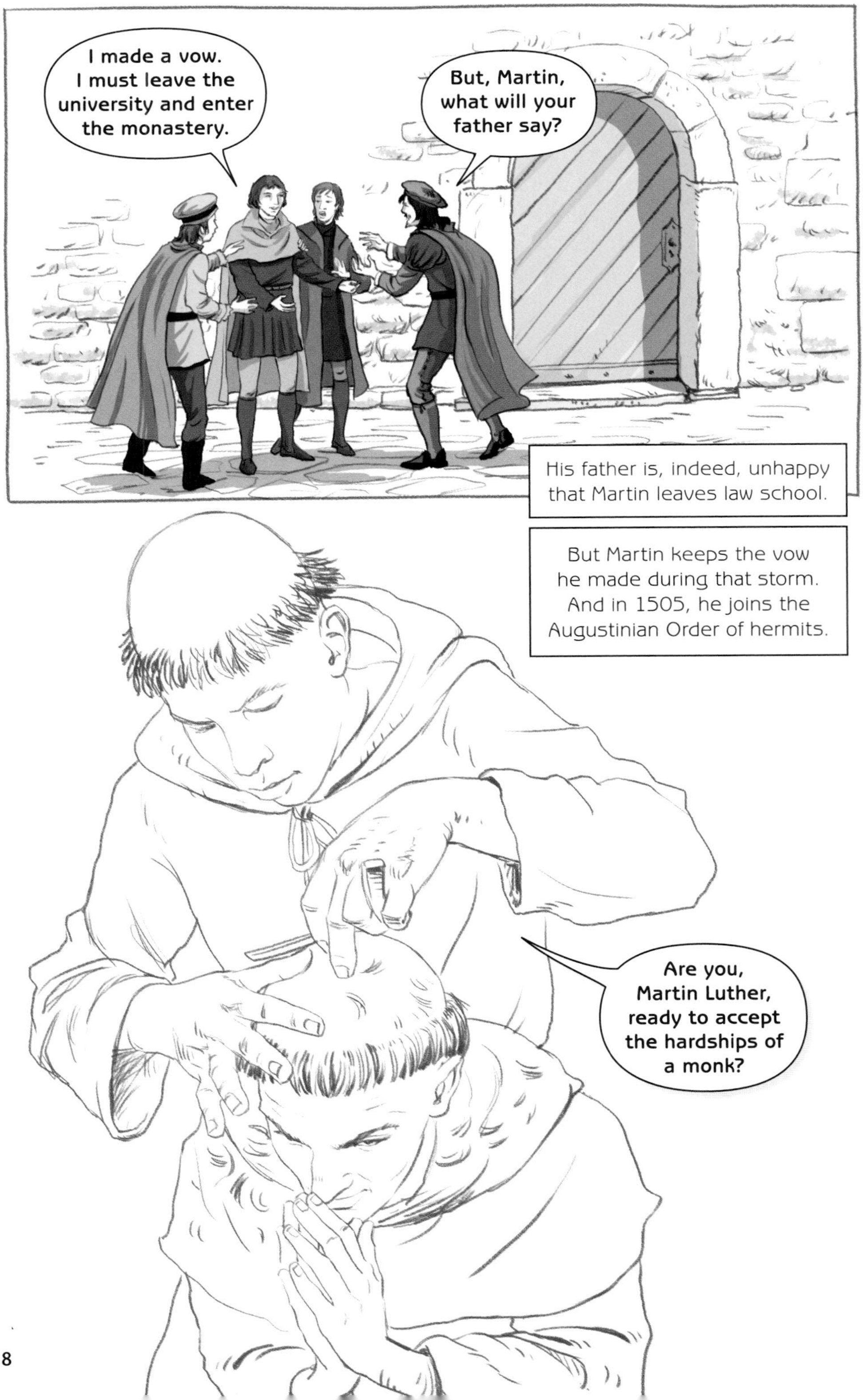

I made a vow. I must leave the university and enter the monastery.
But, Martin, what will your father say?
His father is, indeed, unhappy that Martin leaves law school.
But Martin keeps the vow he made during that storm. And in 1505, he joins the Augustinian Order of hermits.
Are you, Martin Luther, ready to accept the hardships of a monk?

For the next year, Luther studied, prayed, and worshiped in chapel seven times a day. He was allowed to speak only at certain times. He vowed to never marry, and he gave up all of his personal possessions.

Soon after he became a monk, Luther was chosen to become a priest. He spent the next two years preparing for the priesthood, and on April 3, 1507, he was ordained. Among the worshipers at his first Communion service (or Mass) on May 2 was his father. Although Hans Luther was still not convinced that Martin had made a wise career move, he gave a generous gift for the cloister.

Despite his studies, despite long hours of reading the Bible, Brother Luther struggled with the problem of sin and worried about

earning forgiveness from God.

Brother Martin goes back to the University of Erfurt to continue his schooling. A year later, he accepts a teaching post at the University of Wittenberg. There, in addition to teaching, Luther also continues his studies of the Bible and the Early Church.

His worries about sin linger. And nothing, not even the comforting words of his advisor, eases his mind.

Remember the Creed, Brother Martin: "I believe in the forgiveness of sins."

Luther earned a bachelor's degree at Wittenberg in 1509 and returned to Erfurt, this time to teach at the university. And he continued to study, earning two more degrees.

When he was chosen to go to Rome on church business, Martin was thrilled! In Rome, he hoped to finally find answers to the

questions that still troubled him.

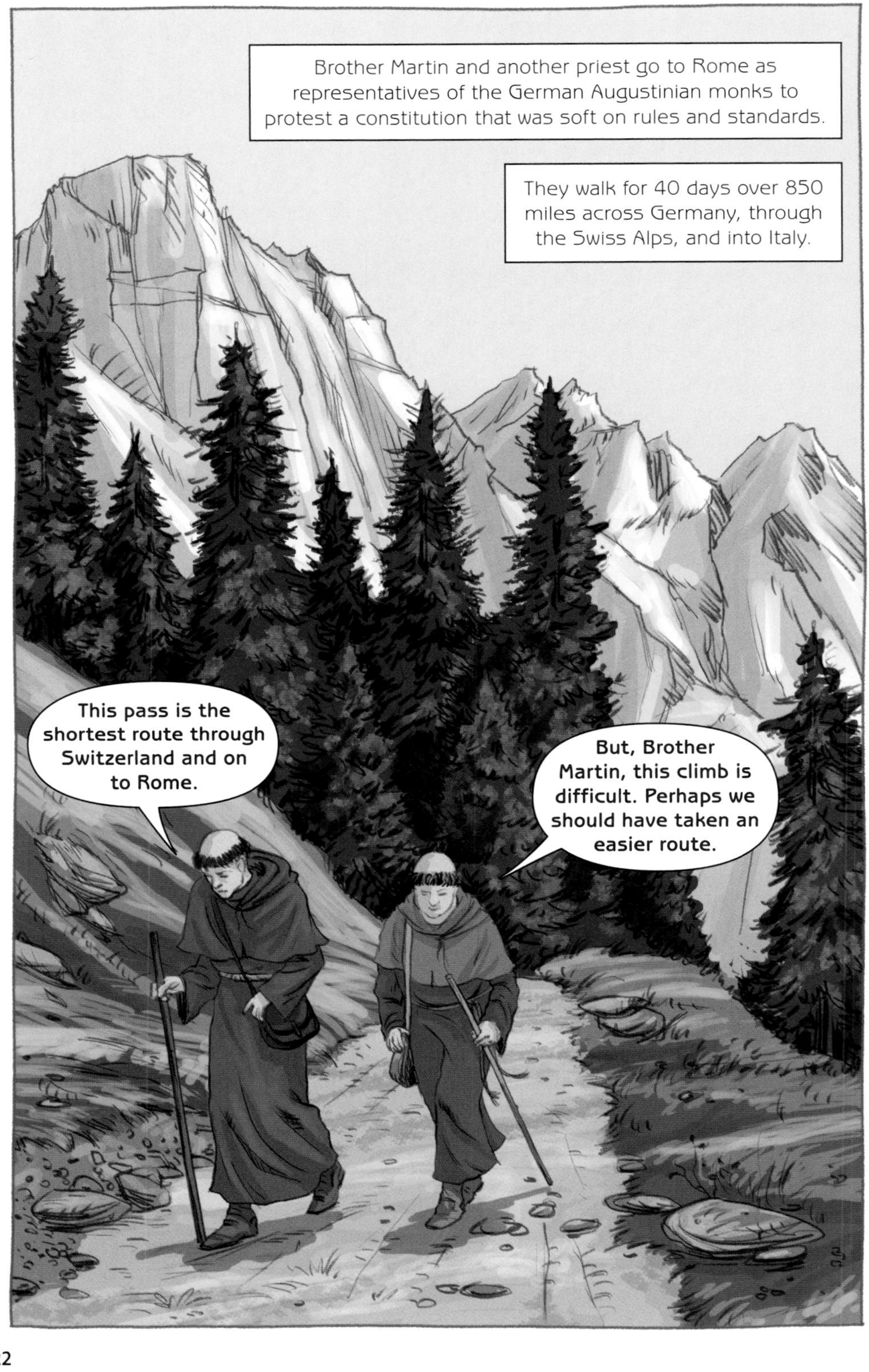
Brother Martin and another priest go to Rome as representatives of the German Augustinian monks to protest a constitution that was soft on rules and standards.
They walk for 40 days over 850 miles across Germany, through the Swiss Alps, and into Italy.
This pass is the shortest route through Switzerland and on to Rome.
But, Brother Martin, this climb is difficult. Perhaps we should have taken an easier route.

While he is in Rome, Luther explores the city. He visits many churches and historic sites, and he climbs the 28 steps that legend said Jesus climbed as He was taken to Pilate.

Rome, the capital of the great Roman Empire, was more than 2,000 years old at the time of Luther's visit. There were 70 monasteries and dozens of churches in the city in those days. There were caves, called *catacombs*, where people were buried. And, because Rome was the cultural and religious capital of Europe, there were many artists, poets, and priests.

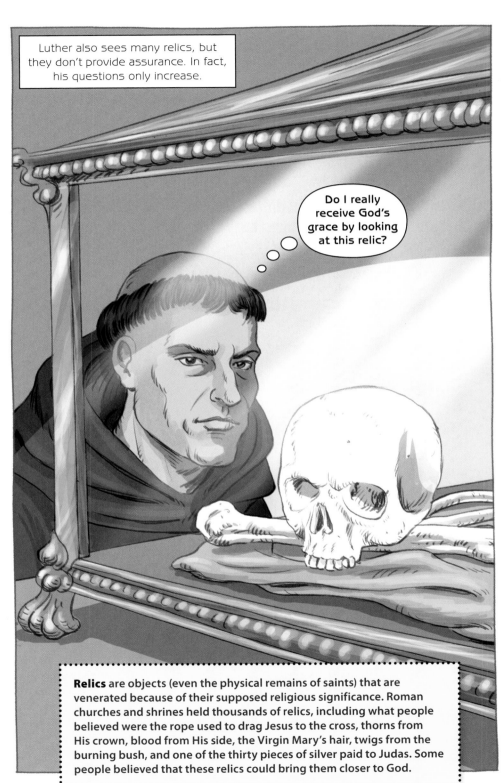

Luther also sees many relics, but they don't provide assurance. In fact, his questions only increase.

Do I really receive God's grace by looking at this relic?

Relics are objects (even the physical remains of saints) that are venerated because of their supposed religious significance. Roman churches and shrines held thousands of relics, including what people believed were the rope used to drag Jesus to the cross, thorns from His crown, blood from His side, the Virgin Mary's hair, twigs from the burning bush, and one of the thirty pieces of silver paid to Judas. Some people believed that these relics could bring them closer to God.

After a month of on-and-off discussions with the leader of the Augustinian order, their request for a strict constitution was not approved. Discouraged, Luther and the other monk left Rome and walked back through the Alps to Germany.

Back in Erfurt, in March 1511, Luther resumed studying and teaching. But he is troubled by memories of

what he saw and heard in Rome.

That summer, John Staupitz calls Martin back to Wittenberg, which now becomes his permanent home.

At the university, Luther continues to teach and to study. In 1512, he earns a doctor of theology degree.

Beloved, you are declared righteous by the Gospel!

Soon, Luther is the official preacher of the monastery, and he delivers his sermons in an old wooden chapel. When he begins preaching publicly, his sermons are so popular with the townspeople that he moves to a larger church, the Town Church, where there is room for everyone.

And so began Luther's career as a professor of the Bible at the widely respected University of Wittenberg.

These were formative years for young

Professor Luther.

In addition to his lectures, he was responsible for supervising the monastery's beginning students, called novices. He was also responsible for overseeing eleven Augustinian monasteries throughout the region. And he continued to study the Bible.

To be well prepared for his lectures, Luther read closely, being careful to get the right meaning of God's Word. As is so often the case, the teacher learns along with the student. And for Luther, the turning point came as . . .

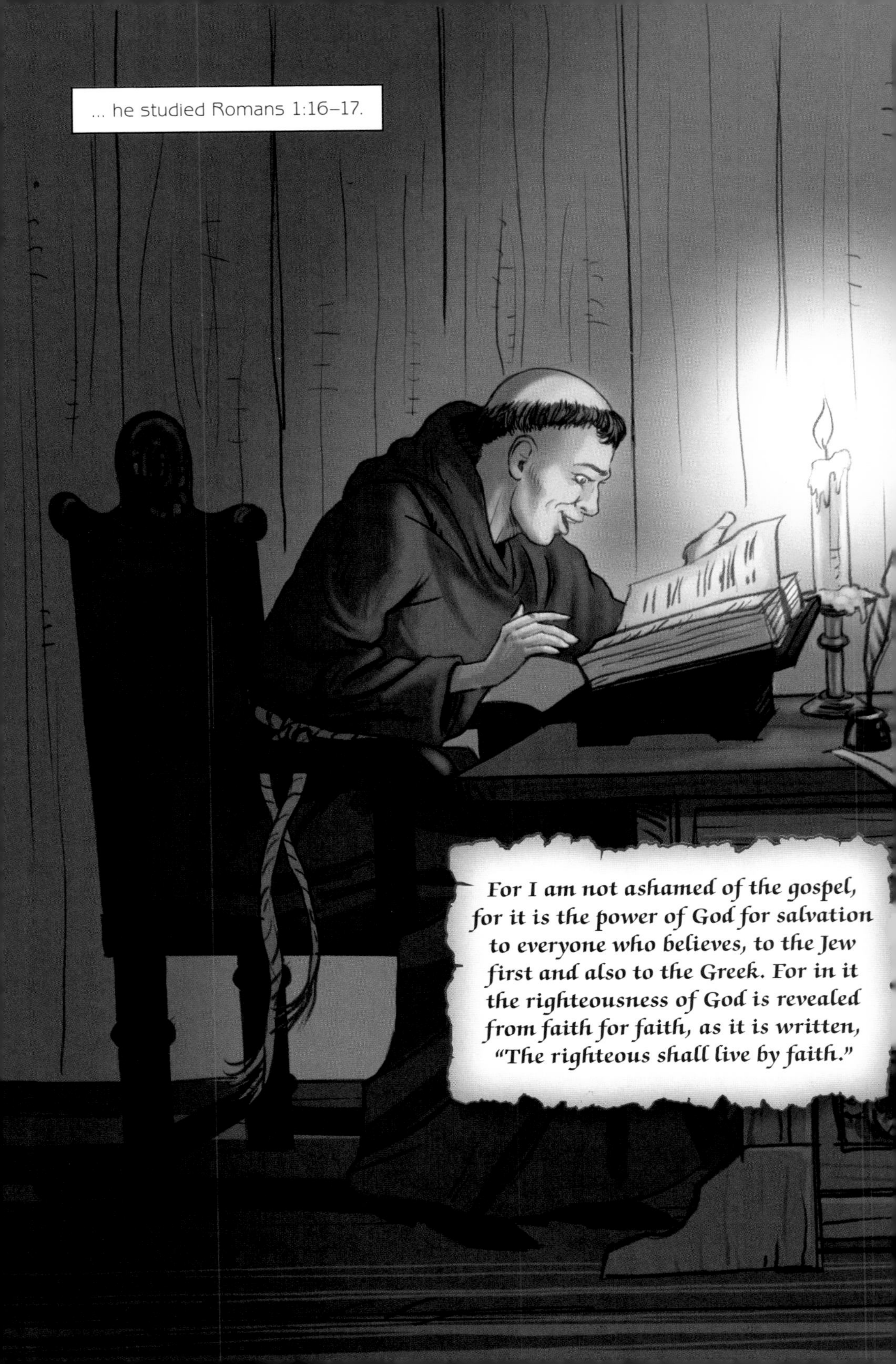
... he studied Romans 1:16–17.
For I am not ashamed of the gospel, for it is the power of God for salvation to everyone who believes, to the Jew first and also to the Greek. For in it the righteousness of God is revealed from faith for faith, as it is written, "The righteous shall live by faith."

Martin Luther had, for years, been tormented by the question, "How can I be sure that God forgives my sin and loves me?" Now he knew the answer to that question.

In the pages of his Bible, he discovered the Gospel message that Jesus took the punishment for our sins in our place.

This was Martin Luther's great

"Tower Experience."

That moment of understanding gave him the peace and assurance of God's forgiveness he had been searching for.

∽

At this time in German history, the church was led by Joachim, an elector from Brandenburg, and his brother, Albert, who was bishop of Halberstadt and archbishop of both Magdeburg and Mainz. To get these jobs, these men contributed millions of dollars to the church in Rome.

But because neither Albert nor Joachim had this much money, they borrowed it from a family of bankers. Loans must be paid back, of course, and Pope Leo allowed Albert to raise money to pay this loan by selling **indulgences**. Half of the money they received from selling indulgences went to pay their debt to the bankers, and the rest went to Rome to help pay for the building of the Basilica of St. Peter.

Electors were powerful men, second only to the emperor. There were seven electors who either inherited their position or were appointed by the pope. Electors chose who would be the next Holy Roman Emperor, and the pope made this choice official when he crowned the emperor.

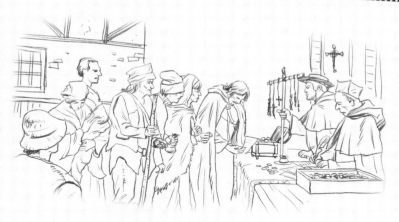

▪ Indulgences

The simple definition of *penance* is repentance from sin. A Christian who does penance is truly sorry for his sin, confesses it, and is forgiven by faith in Jesus Christ. In the Catholic Church, penance includes absolution by a priest, prayer, doing good works, and indulgences. A person can do penance to reduce or remove punishment for sins while he lives on earth and in purgatory after death.

Purgatory is a Catholic belief that faithful people who die may not be ready for heaven, so they spend time in a "between place" of temporary punishment for their sins.

Sometimes people can do penance by contributing money to build a church or a hospital, for example. Beginning in the eleventh century, this contribution took the form of indulgence letters that people could purchase. In Luther's time, Pope Leo allowed the sale of indulgences to raise money for, among other things, an army to defend the church from its enemies within the church and without (namely, the Ottoman Empire).

Albert couldn't go door-to-door to sell indulgences himself. So, with Pope Leo's approval, Albert chose a monk named John Tetzel to do the selling to the German people for him. This would give Albert the money he needed to repay his large debts, it would give the pope the money he needed to build his magnificent church in Rome, and in the mind of the people, it would give them the indulgences they thought they needed to

buy forgiveness.

It would seem that this would make everyone happy. But that was not the case. Like Joachim, Frederick the Wise was also an elector in Germany, and he was very influential. Frederick did not want Tetzel coming into his country to sell indulgences because he was selling them there himself. Frederick wanted people to keep their money in Germany and not send it to Rome.

A contrite heart, sincere repentance, and the Gospel of Jesus Christ are what is important for your soul—not the purchase of indulgences!

Martin Luther preached against indulgences.

And all this interest in them bothered him because they were a scam! Luther preached that the only way to avoid hell and go to heaven was through Christ, not through people's own efforts, and certainly not through buying a

Yet the selling of indulgences went on.

Luther hoped to put an end to the practice by drawing attention to it. He wrote a list of objections to indulgences, called the

Ninety-five Theses,

and he posted this list on the door of the Castle Church in Wittenberg. The doors were like a community bulletin board, and his action was meant to open up his concerns to public discussion.

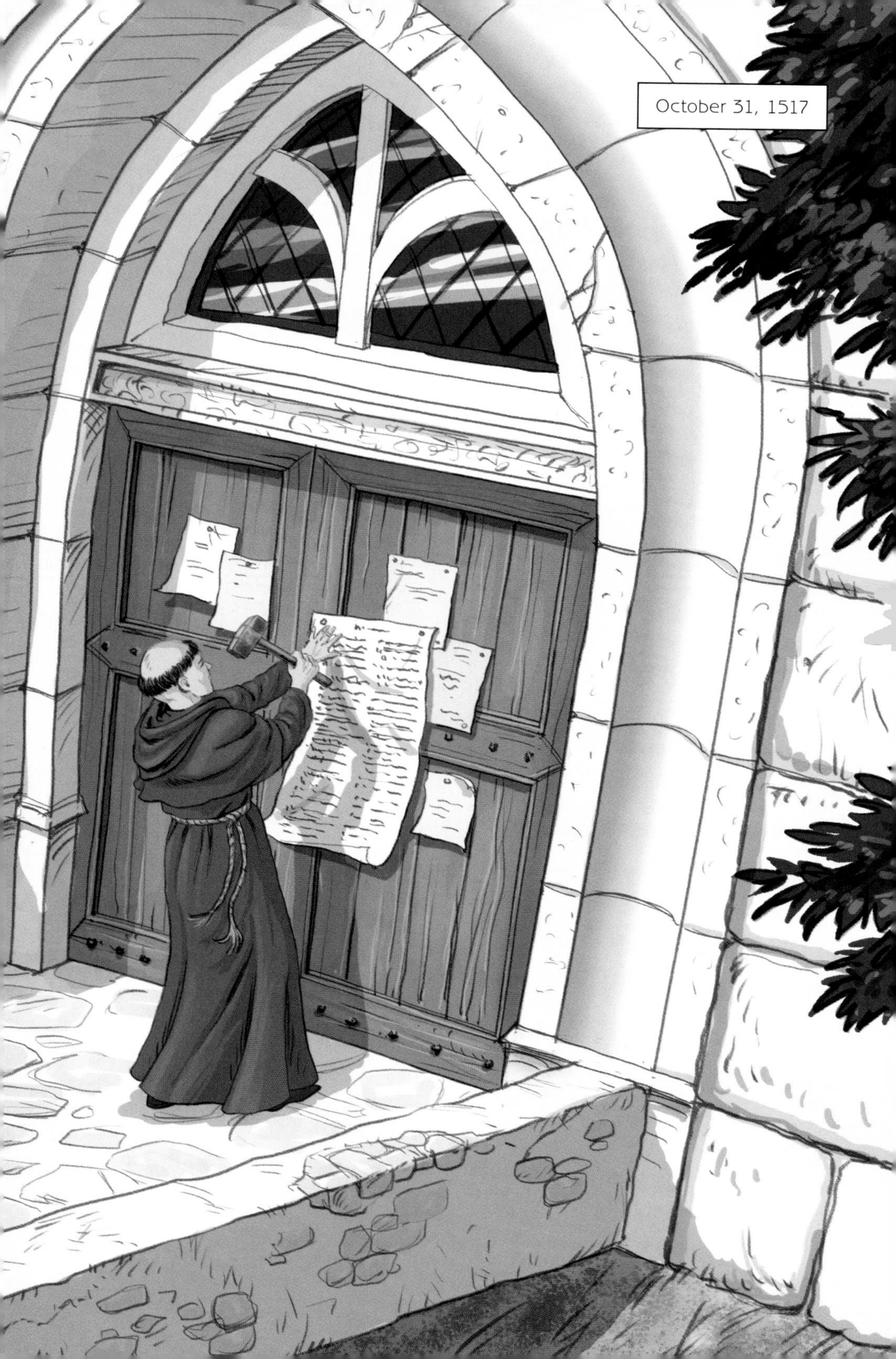
October 31, 1517

" If he have faith, the believer cannot be restrained. . . . He breaks out. He confesses and teaches this gospel to the people at the risk of life itself. "

❖ **Luther the Heretic**

Martin Luther

■ Who's that again?

So many names! Are you wondering who all these people are and how they fit with the story of Martin Luther and the Reformation? Some people, as we've already seen, were clearly on the side of the reformers; others were definitely against them. Still others just stood back and waited to see how it would end.

ALLIES

Frederick the Wise—German leader; one of seven electors in the Holy Roman Empire. (See p. 45.)

Philip Melanchthon—Luther's closest ally. He was the author of the Augsburg Confession. (See p. 117.)

Katharina von Bora—a former nun who learned of Luther through his writings. Katie and Martin married in 1525 and had six children. She died in 1552, the result of injuries after falling from a wagon as she left Wittenberg to avoid the bubonic plague.

John the Steadfast—became elector after Frederick's death. (See p. 99.)

Lucas Cranach—painter, druggist, and printer; he painted portraits of nearly all of the important reformers. (See p. 89.)

George Spalatin—secretary to Frederick; he was Luther's good friend and go-between with Frederick.

John Staupitz—vicar of the Augustinians in Wittenberg; he was Luther's confessor and close friend.

Andreas Carlstadt—faculty member with Luther at Wittenberg; he debated Eck at Leipzig.

Frederick the Wise

Katharina von Bora

Lucas Cranach

ADVERSARIES

Charles V—elected as emperor, he was the reigning monarch of the realm of the church in Germany. (See p. 70.)

John Tetzel—a Dominican monk who traveled to preach, he led the sale of indulgences in Germany.

John Calvin—although his early work reflected Luther's influence, Calvin disagreed with Lutheran doctrine. He founded the Protestant Church in Switzerland.

Thomas de Vio Cajetan—a cardinal, he interviewed Luther at the Diet of Augsburg.

Leo X—pope from 1513 to 1521, he excommunicated Luther and authorized the sale of indulgences to fund the building of St. Peter's. Leo struggled with finances (his own and those of the church), and led the Catholic Church during the Reformation.

John Eck—theologian who debated Carlstadt and Luther; he was Luther's prosecutor at the Diet of Worms and was responsible for writing most of the document that excommunicated Luther.

Ulrich Zwingli—a Swiss reformer; he and Luther clashed over the doctrine of the Lord's Supper. (See p. 123.)

Henry VIII—although he was very interested in the change Luther brought about and how it would affect the church in his own country, Henry opposed Luther and had his writings burned in England.

Emperor Charles V

Cardinal Cajetan

Pope Leo X

John Eck

Luther didn't stop at the church door in Wittenberg.

He wanted the church leaders throughout Germany to understand his sincere concerns about indulgences and to respond to them. So he sent copies of the Ninety-five Theses to Albert, the archbishop of Mainz, and to Bishop Schulze of Brandenburg.

Albert (an Augustinian monk, like Luther) was unhappy with Luther's comments. After all, it was his decision to have Tetzel sell indulgences, so Luther's Theses criticized him personally. The Theses also criticized the pope, since he approved of indulgences. So Albert sent Luther's list to the church leaders in Rome to inform them.

Tetzel (a Dominican priest) was just as unhappy with Luther because the theses were targeted at him too. Tetzel vowed to have Luther "burned and his ashes scattered on the waters." Tetzel wrote to his Dominican leaders in Rome and asked them to help silence Luther.

Albert and Tetzel call for immediate action against Luther. But the Roman Curia (those men who help the pope run the church) are cautious when they receive their copy of Luther's Theses. No one wants trouble, but they do take notice.

We cannot afford more discord in the church.

Rather than reacting strongly the way Albert and Tetzel do, Pope Leo sends a message to John Staupitz, Luther's mentor in Wittenberg, telling him to suppress Luther's criticisms.

Deliver this to Staupitz right away!

A general meeting of the Augustinian order was already scheduled to be held in Heidelberg. The Dominican and Roman leaders hoped that would be enough to hush him up.

Luther has no trouble as he walks the 270 miles to Heidelberg, despite Tetzel's threats against his life and Albert's call for his arrest.

Because Luther's original list was printed and widely distributed throughout Germany, more and more people read his statements and began to question the church's practice of indulgences.

In Heidelberg, Luther's fellow Augustinians were receptive to his explanation of his now famous document. In fact, rather than telling him to stop, they asked for more information. He was happy to comply. Luther returned to Wittenberg to write a more in-depth explanation of his Theses and to continue teaching his beliefs.

But in Rome, the Dominicans were not satisfied, and the Curia began to believe that Luther was dangerous. They demanded that he come to Rome so they could interrogate him face-to-face.

Tension about Luther's writings increased in Germany too. Some of Tetzel's friends had written two documents that were very critical of the church leaders and their practices—and they signed Luther's name to them. Pope Leo believed that Luther had written these documents, so, with Emperor Maximilian's full knowledge, he declared Luther a **heretic** and ordered him arrested.

> A **heretic** is someone who no longer believes or teaches as the church does. This is a serious charge to make against a priest and university professor!

Now, Luther's life was in danger!

The charge of heresy was a serious one, but the Roman Curia would drop it if Luther would recant—that is, take back what he wrote and preached.

This Luther would not do; he had to defend the truth he read in the Bible. Luther called on Prince Frederick the Wise to intervene on his behalf. Frederick agreed to protect Luther and to make sure he was treated fairly. Frederick was a powerful ally—an ally that Pope Leo also wanted.

Leo needed all the political and financial support he could get. The Ottoman Empire was gaining ground in Africa and the Mediterranean, and posed a constant threat to Rome as well. The pope needed money to equip his army. He also needed money to continue the construction on the cathedral. Therefore, to maintain Frederick's financial support, Leo went along with what he wanted—which was to keep Luther safe in Germany.

Luther still had to answer for his Ninety-five Theses, though. And Pope Leo agreed to let him defend himself before Cardinal Cajetan in Augsburg.

■ Frederick the Wise
Elector of Saxony

The son of an elector and son-in-law of a duke, Frederick III was powerful in politics and influential in the church. He was recognized as a peacekeeper and was committed to education, founding Wittenberg University, which was the home of the Reformation. Although Frederick had little personal contact with Martin Luther, he sympathized with the reformers and is best known for protecting Luther against those who wanted to arrest him.

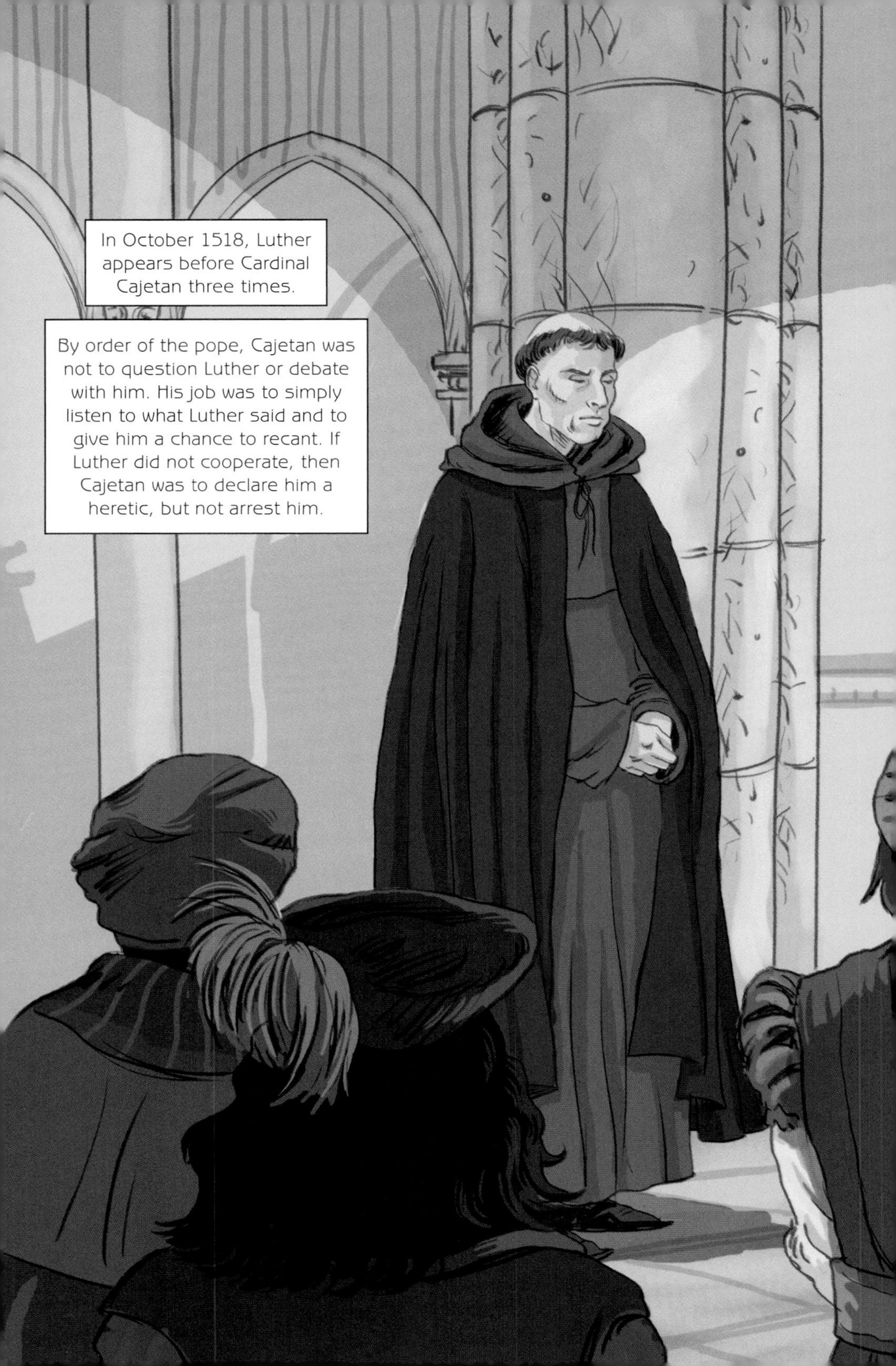
In October 1518, Luther appears before Cardinal Cajetan three times.
By order of the pope, Cajetan was not to question Luther or debate with him. His job was to simply listen to what Luther said and to give him a chance to recant. If Luther did not cooperate, then Cajetan was to declare him a heretic, but not arrest him.

But at each of the three meetings, Cajetan demanded that Luther recant. And each time he refused.

The angry cardinal turned to John Staupitz, Luther's mentor, and told him to make Luther recant. To smooth things over, Staupitz convinced Luther to write a letter of apology to Cajetan. Luther did, saying he was sorry for losing his temper—but not for his beliefs and writings.

He did not recant.

By this time, rumors spread that Cajetan was so angry he wanted both Staupitz and Luther to be arrested. Staupitz leaves Augsburg immediately.

Find those men!

Luther stays long enough to write a letter to Pope Leo, saying that if someone could point out where the Bible said he was wrong, then he would recant.

Martin, they are after you. Make haste!

Thank you, friends!

Then, at the urging of his friends, Luther leaves Augsburg under the cover of night.

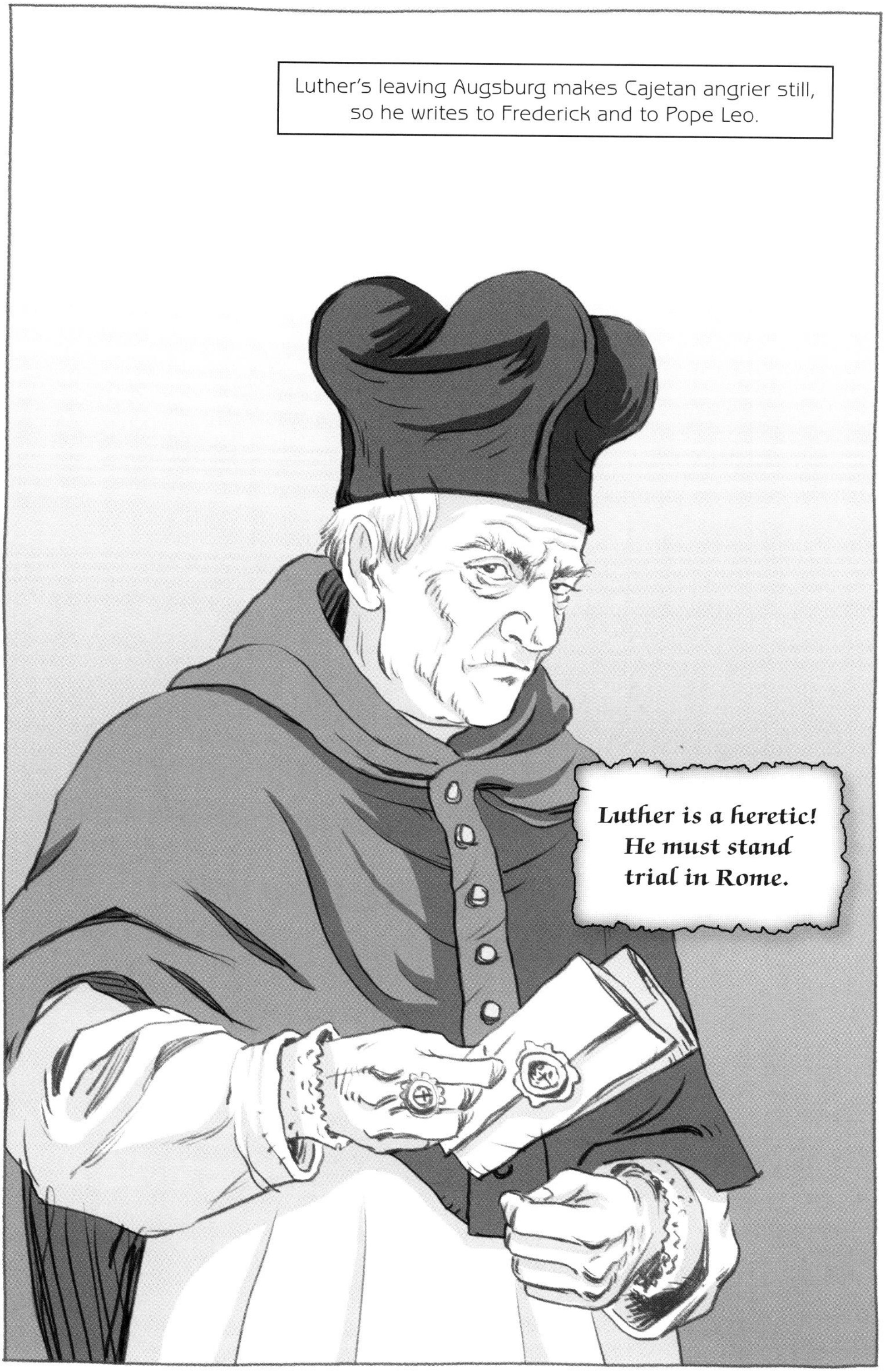
Luther's leaving Augsburg makes Cajetan angrier still, so he writes to Frederick and to Pope Leo.
Luther is a heretic! He must stand trial in Rome.

When Luther learns about these letters, he writes a pamphlet stating his version of the issue and asking other church leaders to join the discussion. But Luther makes this request without the pope's permission, which violates church policy.

What do Prince Frederick and other church leaders have to say?

There are two sides to this difficult situation.

Frederick wants to keep Luther out of trouble, but as a leader in the church, he is responsible for following church rules.

Frederick writes two letters. First, he asks Emperor Maximilian to either drop the whole matter or at least say that Luther can stay in Germany and not have to go to Rome for trial.

Then he writes to Cajetan …

I will not send Luther to Rome unless he is clearly proven a heretic.

But Cajetan's letter to Pope Leo got there first. Leo agreed with Cajetan's remarks about Luther and about indulgences, so he made Cajetan's statements the official opinion of the church. Leo added that anyone who taught differently would be excommunicated.

Martin Luther, of course, taught differently.

Luther wasn't Pope Leo's only problem, as we know. As doctrinal debates in Germany continued, political issues in Rome were also on the rise.

In addition to his need for money and the threat of war, Leo knew that Emperor Maximilian I was at the end of his life and soon a new emperor would be elected. Because he couldn't afford to lose Frederick's support over something like Luther's writings, Leo tried a different tactic. He sent **Karl von Miltitz**, a German and a relative of Frederick, as his special representative to Frederick.

Miltitz brought with him special gifts from the pope himself. There were generous indulgences for the Castle Church in Wittenberg (where Luther preached). And there was the Golden Rose of Virtue as a gift of honor for Frederick. The pope personally blessed the rose and awarded it once a year to just one important person. Pope Leo and his friends no doubt thought these honors would keep Frederick on their side.

Miltitz was in for a surprise. He arrived in Germany, bearing his gifts and expecting that Frederick would hand Luther over to him. But he soon learned that many people agreed with Luther. He also learned that

Frederick had no intention of sending Luther to Rome.

Still, Frederick was loyal to the church and he wanted to cooperate. Therefore, he arranged a meeting between Miltitz and Luther.

That meeting lasted two days. At the end of it, Miltitz agreed to write to the pope with a request for a review of Luther's writings to identify any biblical errors.

And Luther agreed to two things. First, he would stop preaching and writing against indulgences if Tetzel and Albert would stop complaining about him. Second, he would recant if it were found that his writings were not in agreement with the Bible.

Luther was wary, though:

"We separated peaceably, with a kiss (a Judas kiss!) and tears—

I pretended that I did not know they were crocodile tears."

Before he returns to Rome, Miltitz meets with John Tetzel. Miltitz denounces Tetzel as a trouble maker, and Tetzel loses the support of his friends.

When Luther hears about this, he writes to Tetzel.

Don't take it too hard. You didn't start this racket.

John Tetzel dies, alone and deserted, a few months later.

Upon his return to Rome, Miltitz reported to Pope Leo, providing a misleadingly positive account of his meetings in Germany. Leo wrote a warm "welcome back" letter to Luther, saying he was happy that Luther was ready to recant. He even offered to pay Luther's travel expenses to Rome so he could recant there.

Leo was, no doubt, relieved to be done with the Luther issue because he had more pressing things to deal with: Holy Roman Emperor Maximilian I had died and his successor had to be elected.

This election was tricky business for Leo. He desperately wanted the next emperor to be someone he could count on for financial and political support. He hoped that Frederick the Wise or one of the other German electors would be elected to the position. Above all, he did not want King Charles of Spain to be chosen.

But on June 28, 1519, Charles was elected as the new emperor of the Holy Roman Empire. And for the time being, because both the pope and the emperor were preoccupied with other matters,

Martin Luther
was safe.

After the meeting with Karl von Miltitz, Luther had agreed that he would stop speaking out against indulgences if his enemies would end their argument against him. But no one was willing to cooperate.

John Eck, a Luther enemy, challenged Andreas Carlstadt, a Luther friend, to a debate that was held at the University of Leipzig. Carlstadt's argument was stronger, but Eck was a much better speaker—so he easily won the debate.

Then, over the next two weeks, Eck and Luther debated face-to-face. Eck argued that church teachings were to be considered the highest authority, even ahead of the Bible.

But Martin Luther put God's Word above everything else. His strong argument gained him support in Germany and with other Bible scholars throughout the rest of Europe,

but it did not make him popular in Rome.

▪ Luther Supporters

Luther had many supporters throughout Europe. One of these was Desiderius Erasmus.

A Dutch priest, scholar and popular author, Erasmus was born in 1466. He was an expert in Greek and Latin, and in 1516 he published an important translation of the New Testament.

Erasmus was critical of the Catholic Church and worked to reform it, but he did not join the movement. However, his writings about free speech and personal freedom were important to Luther and his work.

Albrecht Duerer was famous throughout all of Europe for his paintings, woodcuts, and engravings. He was loyal to Martin Luther, joined the reformers, and helped people understand the Bible and the Christian faith through his art.

Other influential Germans who supported Martin Luther:

Ulrich von Hutten was a soldier, scholar and poet. He was a strong supporter of Luther and the Reformation, and tried to start a crusade against the Catholic Church.

Franz von Sickingen was a wealthy and powerful German knight who offered military protection to Martin Luther. A friend of von Hutten, he declared war against the Catholics.

Martin Luther continued to preach and teach. The more he communicated his beliefs, the more his enemies criticized them. And the more he wrote . . .

In 1520, Martin published three important booklets:

- *An Address to the Christian Nobility of the German Nations*

- *On the Babylonian Captivity of the Church*

- *The Freedom of the Christian Man*

Dramatic changes in technology made all printed materials easier to produce and distribute. This meant that Luther's writings became widely available throughout Europe. Consequently, more and more people read them and were influenced by them. In Germany, the clergy and public alike began to question the church and side with the reformers.

But Luther did not have total support in Germany or among scholars. After examining his writings, two universities (Cologne in Germany and Louvain in Belgium) declare them to be heretical.

Lucas Cranach was more than just a successful painter. His workshop was also licensed as Wittenberg's pharmacy and as a print shop. Cranach's shop printed many of Martin Luther's writings, including his translation of the New Testament.

... Hence it is clear that as the soul needs the Word alone for life and justification, so it is justified by faith alone, and not by any works.

As Luther's booklets were distributed and reports of his meeting with John Eck reached Charles, the new emperor, church leaders were forced to closely examine the situation again.

Pope Leo ordered Carl von Miltitz to go speak with Luther again (which he did on October 19) and to once more encourage him to recant. Of course, Luther did not. And Frederick the Wise made arrangements for Martin Luther to appear before a higher authority—the Diet of Worms.

Not what it sounds like!

No, the **Diet of Worms** has nothing to do with what Luther had for lunch!

In the Roman Empire, *diets* were like congressional sessions in the United States are today. This diet was held from January 28 to May 15, 1521.

Worms, one of the oldest cities in Germany, has existed since before Jesus was born! Its name means "settlement in a watery area." Worms is located on the Rhine River. The city was a center of printing during Luther's time.

But Luther's enemies in Rome do not wait for Worms. On June 15, 1520, Leo issues a statement, called a papal bull. In it, he gives 41 reasons Martin Luther is a heretic and why he should be excommunicated. And he gives Luther 60 days to respond to the charges.

All Christians shall burn Martin Luther's writings. ... No one shall give him aid ...

Luther's response is a sharply worded document called *Against the Evil Bull of the Antichrist.* In it, Luther defends himself, saying the pope should withdraw all the charges against him. If Leo does not, it means that the pope is "possessed and oppressed by Satan." It means, Luther writes, that the pope is attacking Christ.

I will not take back anything. ... Christ will judge whose excommunication will stand.

Sixty days after Pope Leo's bull is published, on December 10, 1520, Martin Luther is declared a heretic. This is the day, the pope says, for all of Europe to burn Luther's writings. But, that morning in Wittenberg …

A crowd waited outside the city gates for the book burning to begin. As soon as the fire was lit, students and university professors threw in books and pamphlets. Then the crowd parted as

Martin Luther stepped forward and threw something into the flames.

It was the pope's bull and a book of church laws! None of the books burned in Wittenberg that day were Luther's as the pope had ordered; what burned were writings of the Roman Church.

Now, after more than two years of conflict with Luther, Pope Leo had run out of patience and wanted the matter settled. On January 3, 1521, he excommunicated Martin Luther. Leo said that he and those who agreed with his writings were not true believers in Christ—heathens. And he called on the new emperor to sign a death warrant for Martin Luther.

This put Charles squarely in the middle of the situation. He had already agreed to give Luther a chance to defend himself at the Diet of Worms. In addition, Luther had many friends throughout Germany who would defend him despite the pope's decree. Charles did not immediately honor the pope's request.

And the German Church officials decided instead to see what would happen in Worms.

Who's that again?

See pages 70–71 for more about Charles.

▪ The Diet of Worms

The Diet of Worms of 1521 is important in world history because that was when the twenty-year-old Charles had his first real experience with the delicate politics of the Holy Roman Empire. As inventions made travel and communication easier, the world was expanding, posing new challenges for the church and its young emperor. Charles needed German money to help pay for his elaborate coronation ceremony and to help pay for the military defense of the Holy Roman Empire. For their part, the German leaders at the Diet expected him to solve ongoing concerns that Maximilian had avoided.

The four-month-long Diet is most famous, though, for one thing: Martin Luther.

" Prayer is a strong wall and fortress of the
church; it is a goodly Christian weapon. "

❖ **Luther the Outlaw**

■ Charles of Spain

Holy Roman Emperor

Who was this man, who at 19 became the most powerful ruler in Europe?

His father, Philip, was ruler of Burgundy, Luxemburg, and the Netherlands and son of Emperor Maximilian I. His mother, Joanna, was the daughter of King Ferdinand and Queen Isabella of Spain. His wife, Isabella, was the daughter of the king of Portugal.

When Charles was six years old, his father died, and Charles assumed the throne. When his grandfather Ferdinand died, Charles also became king of Spain, which included the Spanish colonies in the Americas, the Caribbean, and parts of Asia and Italy. And upon his grandfather Maximilian's death, Charles inherited land in Austria, Bohemia, and Hungary.

Ambitious and determined, Charles wanted to be Holy Roman Emperor as his grandfather Maximilian had been. He was willing to spend as much money as he had to in his campaign to win the election, and his efforts paid off. He was elected in June 1519.

For much of his reign, Charles was preoccupied with war with France and with the constant threat of invasion from the Ottomans. But he was also responsible for extending the Spanish territories in what is now the southwest United States, Mexico, and South America.

In 1555, Charles turned over the throne of Spain to his son. A year later, he resigned as Holy Roman Emperor. Charles died in 1558.

Holy Roman Empire

The Holy Roman Empire existed for about a thousand years.
In the 1500s, it included Germany, Austria, Belgium, Moravia,
The Netherlands, Switzerland, and parts of Italy.

One of Luther's most outspoken enemies at Worms was Girolamo Aleander, the pope's representative. His purpose there was to convince the emperor to condemn Luther as a heretic.

Aleander was a respected scholar and university professor. Some believed him to be the most learned man of the time. But he was not welcomed in Germany.

People booed

as he walked along the streets of Worms. Posters ridiculing him were hung throughout the city. He even feared that his life was in danger. It seemed that nearly everyone in Germany was on Luther's side. This was simply more than he could handle.

Aleander contacted Charles soon after the emperor arrived in Worms and said that he should cancel the meeting with Luther. The pope himself, Aleander said, was the proper authority in this issue.

Charles took Aleander's advice. He was already angry with Luther about his writings and his burning of the pope's bull. And he had other business to attend to, so he withdrew the invitation to Luther to defend himself at the Diet of Worms.

But Frederick the Wise intervened on Luther's behalf once more. After a heated discussion between Frederick and Aleander, Charles changed his mind yet again. After all, he needed Germany's support.

On March 11, the emperor reissued his invitation to Luther to come before the Diet for questioning.

Luther, along with many of his friends and the emperor's herald, traveled 300 miles from Wittenberg to Worms. All along the way, his friends and supporters cheered him on and shouted their encouragement. Wherever he visited, he was the guest of honor. And wherever he preached, the churches overflowed with listeners.

Luther arrived in Worms on April 16, 1521. A watchman in a tower of the cathedral saw him approach and announced his arrival to the waiting crowd.

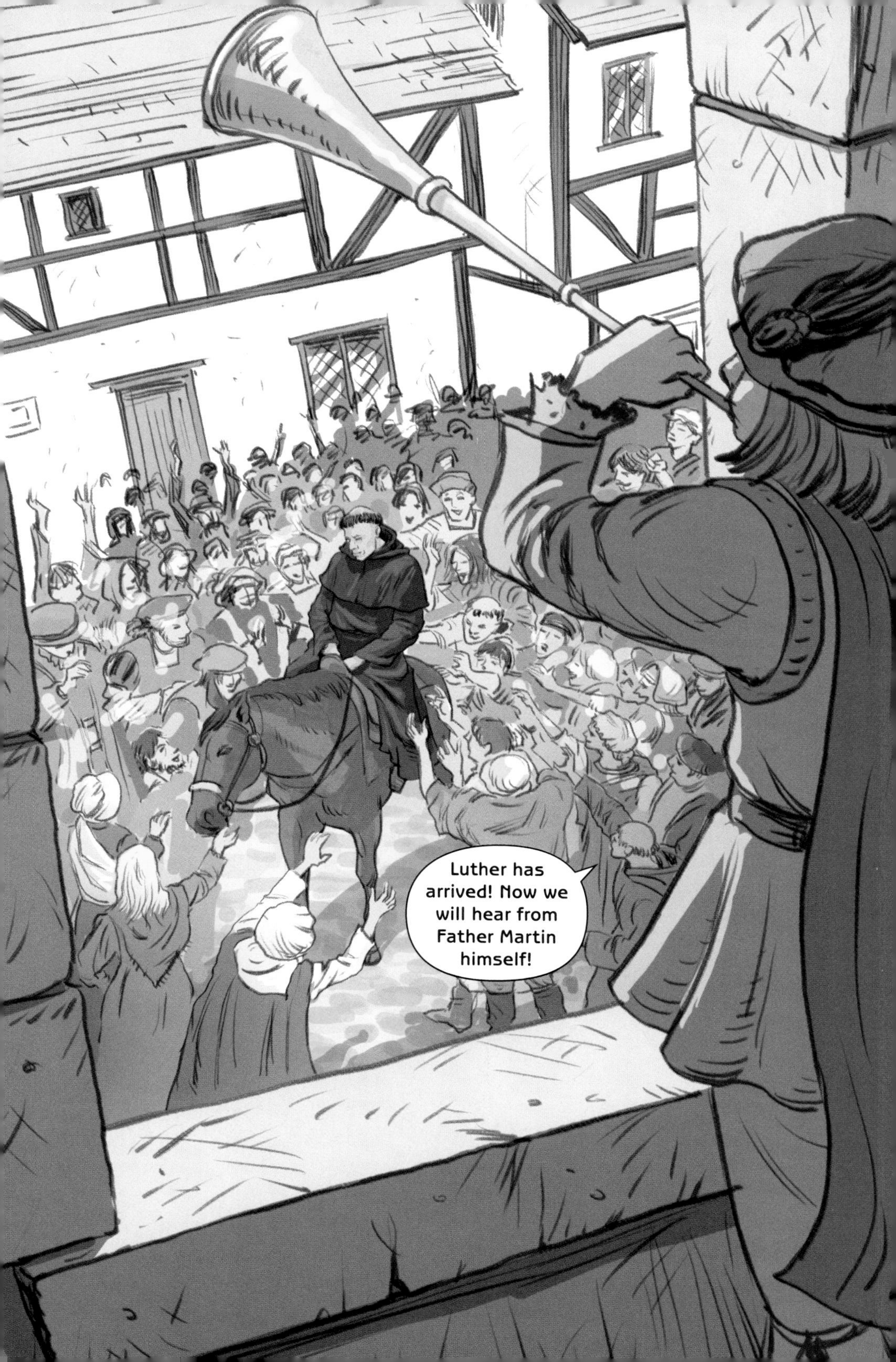
Luther has arrived! Now we will hear from Father Martin himself!

The next afternoon, Martin Luther is led through the backstreets of Worms to a second-floor room of the bishop's palace.

Martin Luther, you must answer only two questions!

Did you write these 25 books?

Do you defend them ... or do you RECANT?

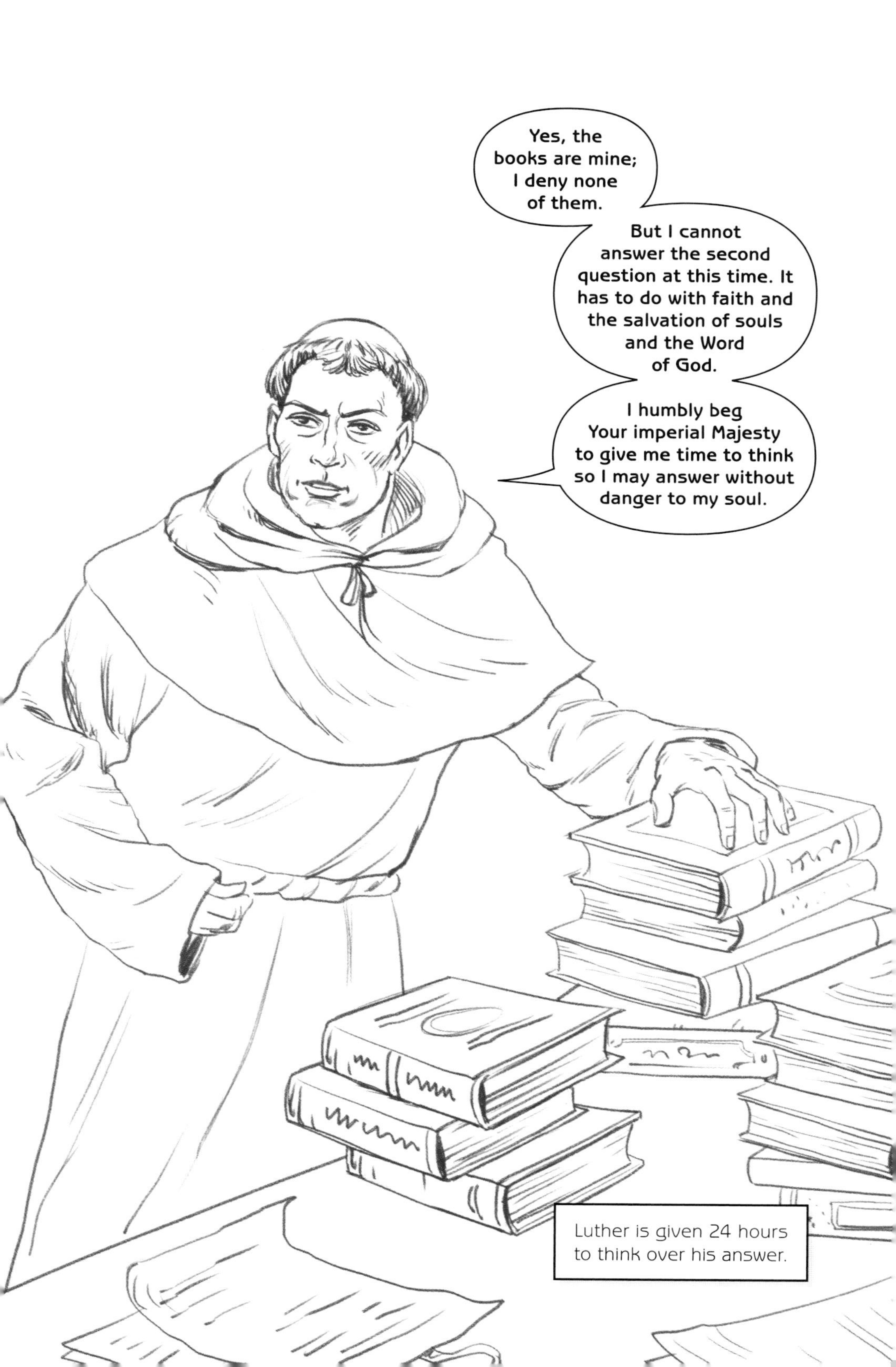
Yes, the books are mine; I deny none of them.
But I cannot answer the second question at this time. It has to do with faith and the salvation of souls and the Word of God.
I humbly beg Your imperial Majesty to give me time to think so I may answer without danger to my soul.
Luther is given 24 hours to think over his answer.

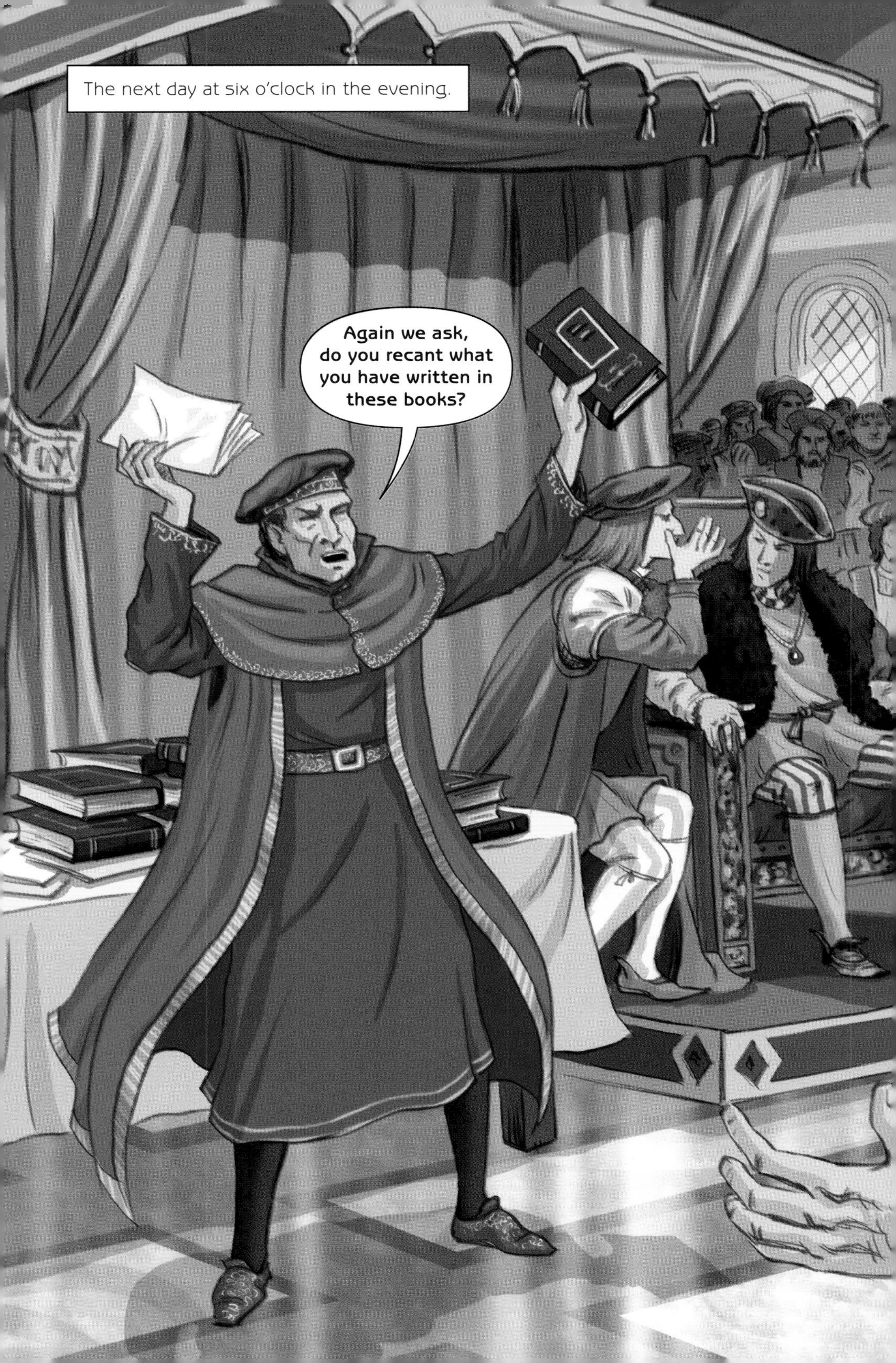
The next day at six o'clock in the evening.
Again we ask, do you recant what you have written in these books?

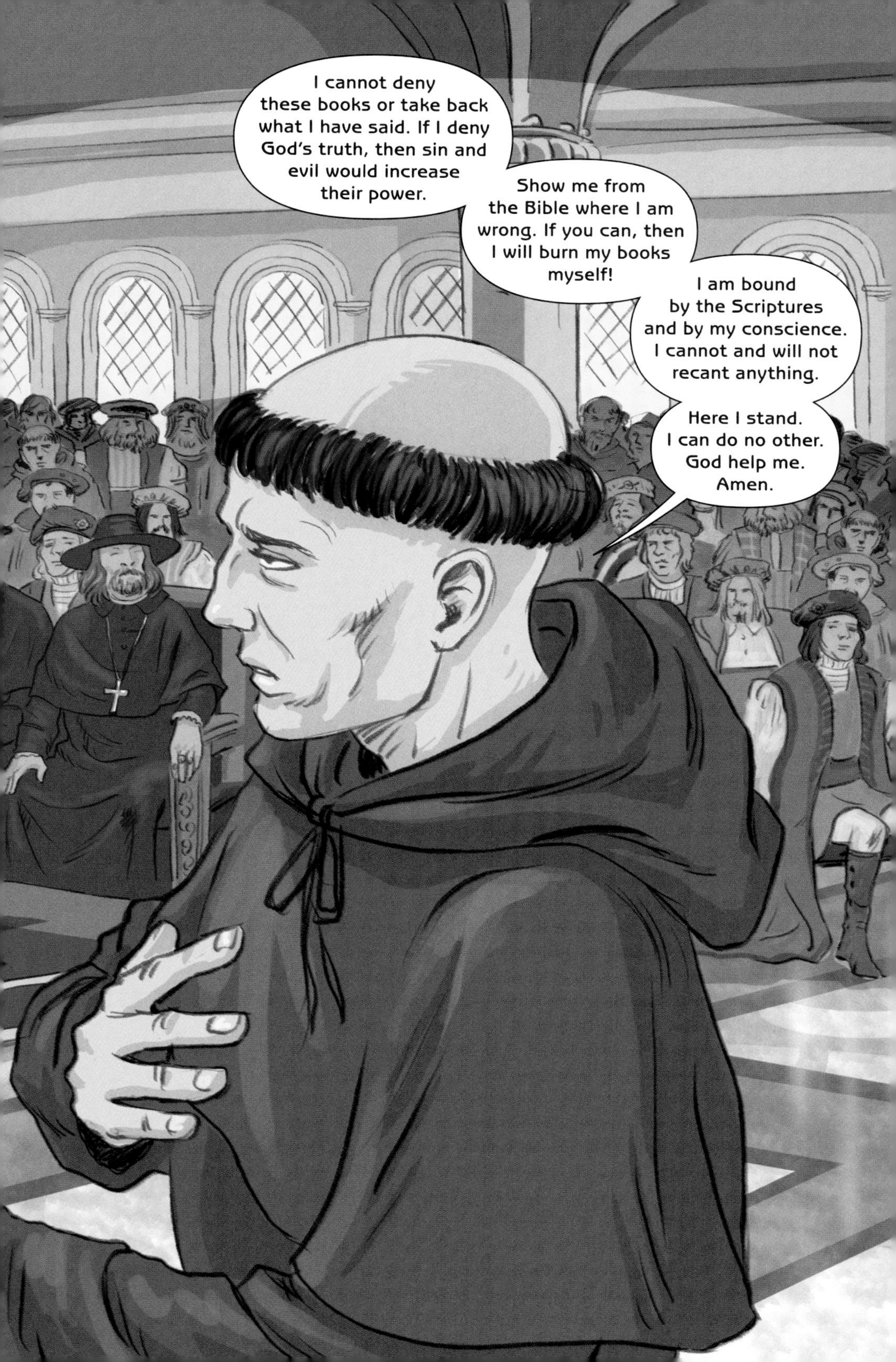
I cannot deny these books or take back what I have said. If I deny God's truth, then sin and evil would increase their power.
Show me from the Bible where I am wrong. If you can, then I will burn my books myself!
I am bound by the Scriptures and by my conscience. I cannot and will not recant anything.
Here I stand. I can do no other. God help me. Amen.

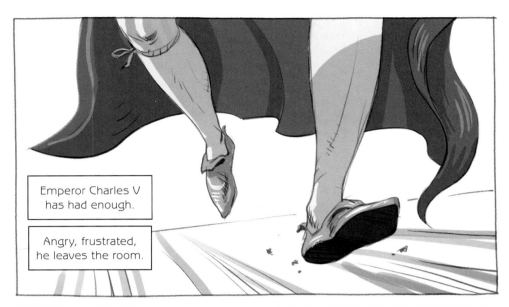

Emperor Charles V has had enough.

Angry, frustrated, he leaves the room.

Luther's friends congratulate him. But the emperor's friends boo and shout.

To the fire with him!

Aleander pressured the emperor to act immediately to declare Luther an outlaw, but Charles was cautious. He spoke with Frederick the Wise and the other German princes, but they were cautious too; they thought condemning Luther might start a war. Next, a committee encouraged Luther to keep the peace by recanting his writings and coming to terms with the church's teachings.

But Luther was firm, saying that he would recant *only* if they could show him in the Bible or "by clear reasoning" where he was wrong.

There was a stalemate.

When he heard this, Charles permitted Luther to leave Worms and promised that he would be safe on his journey home if he stop preaching, teaching, and writing books that criticized the church. But by this time, Charles had had enough.

Just four days later, on May 25, 1521, Emperor Charles issued an official statement called the Edict of Worms.

In this statement, Charles said Luther was a "devil in monk's clothing," claimed he was a notorious criminal, and cut him off from the church.

Martin Luther was now an outlaw.

By law, none of Luther's friends could have anything to do with him—unless it was to arrest him. Anyone who took his side was also to be arrested. It was now illegal to give him shelter or food or to own or even read any of Luther's writings. There was more—the Edict of Worms ordered that Luther was to be killed on sight.

On his last night in Worms, Martin Luther is visited by his friend George Spalatin, who was secretary to Frederick the Wise.

Are you alone, Martin? I have urgent news ...

The next morning, Luther begins his long trip home to Wittenberg. Three days into the journey, he hands two letters to a messenger and tells him to return to Worms.

Deliver these to the emperor and the Diet!

Luther travels through the dense Thuringian Forest on his way home. Suddenly, from out of the depths of the forest, a band of armed horsemen approaches the travelers.

They drag Luther out of the carriage and into the dark woods.

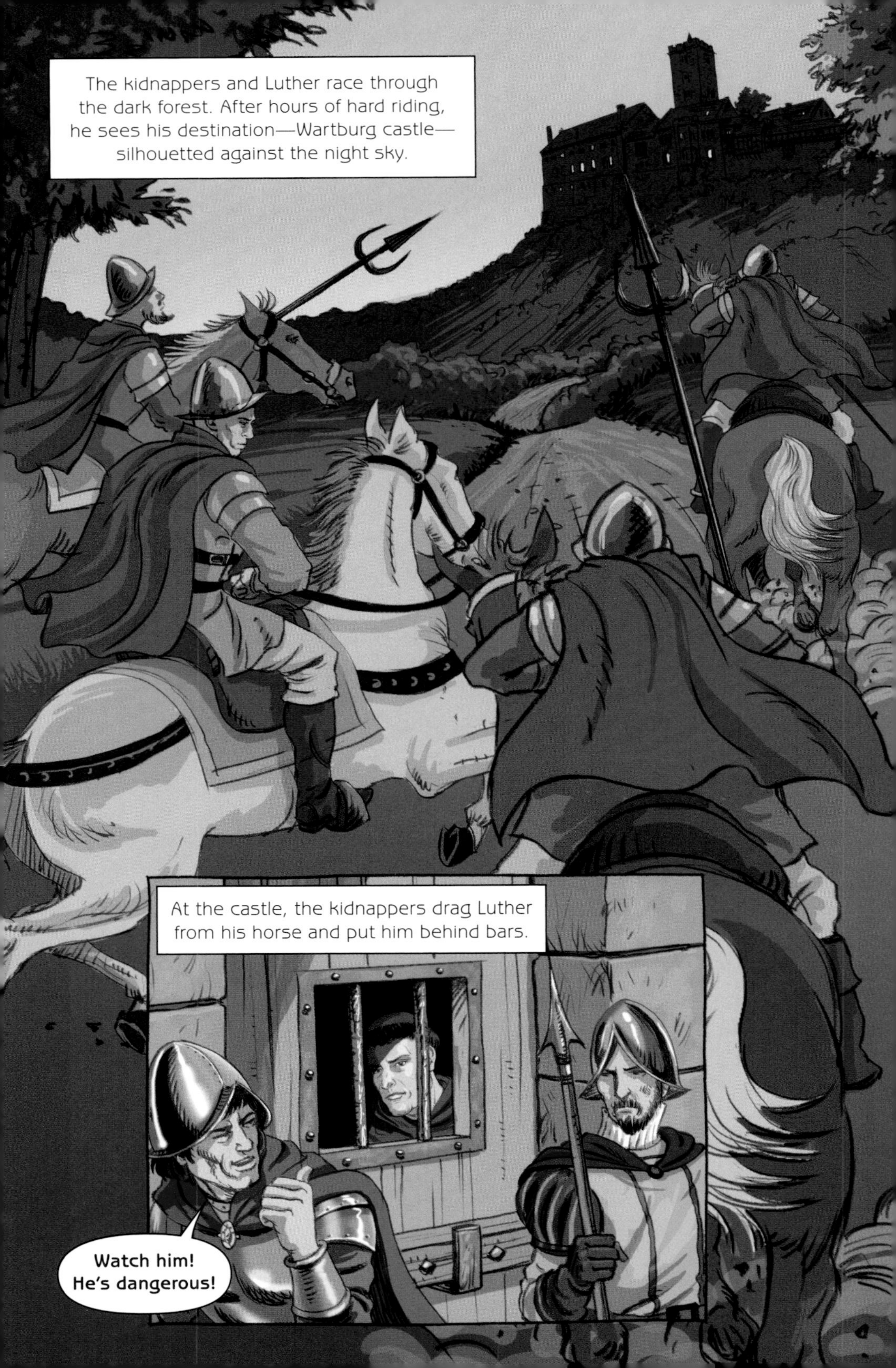
The kidnappers and Luther race through the dark forest. After hours of hard riding, he sees his destination—Wartburg castle—silhouetted against the night sky.
At the castle, the kidnappers drag Luther from his horse and put him behind bars.
Watch him! He's dangerous!

But this was no ordinary kidnapping!

The kidnappers were really his friends, and the fake kidnapping was all part of Frederick's plan to save Martin Luther's life. This was the urgent news that George Spalatin had brought to Luther that last night in Worms.

Luther was now in hiding. Only a few of his friends knew where he was. And because of this secrecy, he was safe.

In this secret hiding place, Luther took off his monk's robes and put on the disguise of a knight. He let his hair and beard grow and no one who saw him knew who he really was.

While he lived at Wartburg castle, he went by the name "Knight George." He kept to himself and seldom left the castle. When he did, for his safety, at least one other man went along to be his bodyguard.

On some occasions, Luther goes to the nearby monastery at Eisenach to study in the library there.

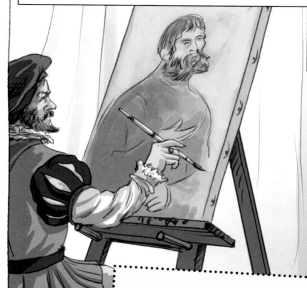

His friends, at least those who know where he is, don't visit because they don't want to jeopardize his safety or their own.

But one man who does come is Lucas Cranach, who paints a famous portrait of "Knight George."

Lucas Cranach the Elder

Discovered by Frederick the Wise, Cranach was his official court painter. Cranach was famous for his woodcuts and portraits. He helped establish the full-length portrait and the Danube style of painting with its lush landscapes. He painted altar pieces for Lutheran and Catholic churches alike, including the altar piece at Wittenberg's town church, St. Mary's, and he created the woodcuts for Luther's translation of the New Testament. It is from Cranach's portraits that we know what Martin Luther and his contemporaries looked like. Cranach's large workshop included an apothecary (pharmacy) and a print shop.

Luther made good use of this quiet time in hiding. Now he had time to devote to Bible study and to write.

During the ten months that he lived at the Wartburg, he composed new pamphlets and books about the errors he found in the church's teaching and practice. But his most significant work there was translating the New Testament into German so that anyone could read the words of Christ.

Finally, the Word of God was available to the German people in their own language.

Luther's edition of the New Testament was illustrated with woodcuts by Lucas Cranach. It became a best-seller almost as soon as it was printed. Now the Word of God was in the hands of the people and not just the priests.

   While Luther was translating and writing, other reformers were busy making changes in the church.

   For example, on Christmas 1521, Andreas Carlstadt began wearing simple black robes instead of the ornate garments of the priests. He spoke German during the Lord's Supper, the first time that many of the 2,000 worshipers there heard these words in a language they knew. Carlstadt also administered the bread *and* the wine during Communion. This was a return to the historic practice that had been abandoned by the Roman Church.

The door to change was open,

but there was confusion about what to do and how much to change. Some priests thought the church was no place for decorations and artwork or even organ music. Vandals destroyed church furnishings and stole artwork. And worse—some priests even began to preach that children should not be baptized or educated and that no one needed a Bible!

The churches in Wittenberg were in turmoil. Everyone was confused. As the weeks passed, the priests and university professors became more and more disheartened.

To settle things, Frederick the Wise appointed a committee to explore what the Bible said about worship practices and churches. But even that committee had trouble coming to agreement.

The one thing everyone agreed upon was this: the only one who could straighten things out was Martin Luther. They wanted him to

come out of hiding.

But that was a problem—he was still an outlaw!

Luther knew how bad things had gotten in Wittenberg because his friends had been keeping him informed in their letters to him. He willingly left his hiding place in Wartburg castle and returned to public leadership of the church. Frederick promised to protect him as well as he could, but the emperor's Edict of Worms was still in effect. Anyone who saw him had permission to arrest him . . . or kill him.

After 10 months in hiding, Luther risks his life and leaves the safety of the castle.

He continues to wear his disguise, though. As Knight George, he safely travels the 150 miles between the castle and Wittenberg.

Back to work, at last!

Luther arrives home on Friday, March 6, 1522.

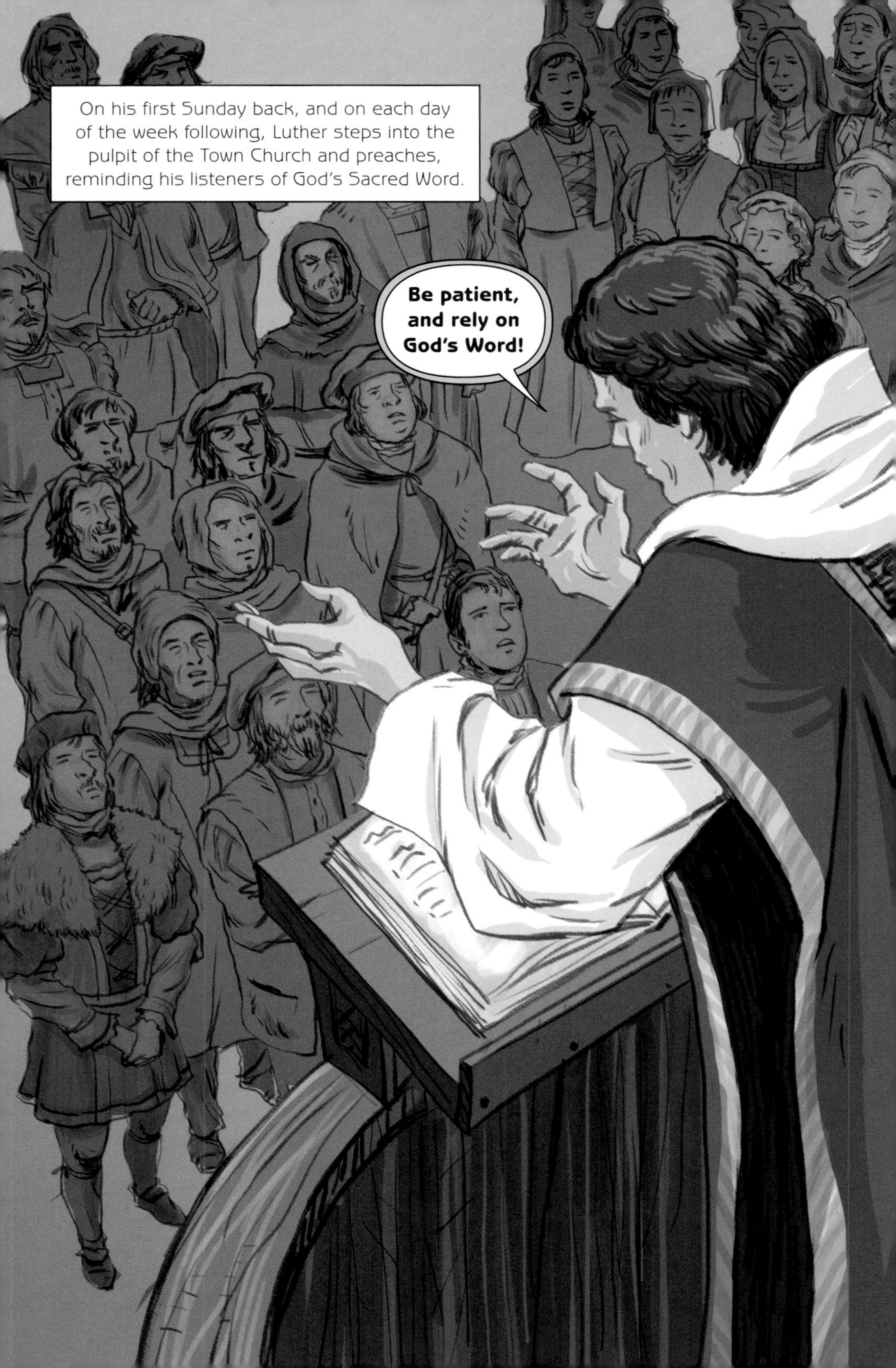
On his first Sunday back, and on each day of the week following, Luther steps into the pulpit of the Town Church and preaches, reminding his listeners of God's Sacred Word.
Be patient, and rely on God's Word!

The people in Wittenberg were relieved to have Luther back home. His leadership soon

restored order.

Mobs stopped harassing monks and priests; churches were once again peaceful and safe places for people to go to. And some of the troublemakers left Wittenberg entirely. Many of them people moved to cities that were outside of Luther's influence and control and adopted false teachings. So the church began to divide and subdivide.

Luther's courage to confront the problems in the Roman Church opened the door for more people to challenge other kinds of oppression. And while taking a stand against what is wrong is considered a brave and good act, it is not always a safe thing to do.

■ The Great Peasants' War

Most German people in the 1500s were peasants. With no education and no real opportunity to change that, they worked and worked, paid more and more taxes, and never, ever got ahead.

Peasant groups had tried uprisings in the past, hoping to improve their condition, but they were not successful. Then, when Luther was effective in challenging the status quo, they were inspired to revolt again—misunderstanding that the change Luther called for was in the context of man's spiritual welfare, not his economic warfare.

There were hundreds of territories in Germany and Austria, and the peasant revolt during the mid-1520s was loosely organized. However, some groups did come together to write a list of requests called the Twelve Articles.

Luther approved of some of the Twelve Articles, but not all of them. He encouraged both the peasants and the German princes to compromise.

But there was too much emotion and too much history between them, and, in 1525, an all-out war ensued. Luther tried to bring about peace, but he failed. Angry and frustrated, he wrote to the German princes, urging them to use force against the peasant uprising. The princes took his advice and sent their armies to kill the peasants.

The war was a disaster: an estimated 100,000 peasants and soldiers died, hundreds of homes and other buildings were destroyed, and Luther lost the support of a great number of his countrymen.

Martin Luther continued to lead the reform of the German Church, but according to the Edict of Worms (remember Worms?), he was to be arrested on sight.

Luther was safe in his own country because he had the support of the German princes. Emperor Charles didn't enforce the edict because he was preoccupied with other matters: his homeland, Spain, was at war with France. But when that war ended in 1526—temporarily—he could focus on other matters. Still, enforcing the edict against Luther didn't happen immediately because there was another Diet. This one, in the city of Speyer, declared that Germans could choose the religion they wanted—Catholic or Lutheran.

But three years later, a second Diet of Speyer reversed that decision and reinforced the Edict of Worms.

Luther and his followers were once more banned from the church.

"But, I Protest!"

People throughout all of Europe had been questioning church practice and policy for centuries. But it wasn't until 1529 the term *Protestant* was first used. During the second Diet of Speyer, German Christians who followed Martin Luther wrote a letter of appeal about the Edict of Worms. Afterward, they were known as Protestants.

▪ John the Steadfast

During the early years of the Reformation, Luther's most powerful friend was Frederick the Wise. Although he was Martin Luther's protector and strong supporter, Frederick was a faithful member of the Roman Church and never officially joined the Lutherans. After Frederick's death in 1525, his brother John succeeded him as elector and, therefore, was in control of the government in Saxony.

John, who was known as "the Steadfast," had been a strong supporter of Luther for many years. After he became elector, he worked fervently to protect Luther and to reform the church, government, and education.

John the Steadfast began his leadership as an elector by examining church affairs in his territory—Saxony. Martin Luther was very involved in this effort, of course, and what he and John learned was disturbing. Some priests were not familiar with even well-known parts of the Bible. And some couldn't even say the Lord's Prayer!

Luther began to publish books about preaching and sermons that were used to train clergy throughout Germany and Europe. Then he wrote a book for families that teaches about the Christian faith:

the Small Catechism, which is still used today.

Luther strongly encouraged all people—young and old, pastors, teachers, parents, servants, everyone!—to read and study the catechism and the Bible.

Luther also reformed the worship service that included the Lord's Supper. This new service was in German— the language of the people—followed Scripture, and encouraged people to sing during the service.

As part of his work for the church, Luther writes many hymns and puts them into a new hymnbook.

Luther had already translated the New Testament into the language of the people. Now he begins translating the Old Testament into German too. This takes 12 years because the original language (Hebrew) is so difficult.

The Hebrew writers do not want to speak in German!

Luther works to reform schools too. He says that all children—girls too!—should learn to read, write, do arithmetic, and study religion. He calls education the responsibility of parents and the government.

" There is no bond on earth so sweet, nor any

separation so bitter, as that which occurs

in a good marriage. "

❖ **Martin and Katie**

Katharina von Bora

—Katie—was born in 1499 on her family's Lippendorf estate (near Leipzig). When her mother died in 1505, she was placed in a convent school in Brehna. When she was 10, she transferred to Marienthron, near Grimma, to live as a nun. Katie took her vows when she was 16.

As part of her preparation to be a nun Katie learned to read and write, which was unusual for most women of that time. Although she did not grow up in a home with loving parents and siblings, Katie had two aunts who also lived at the nunnery: her mother's sister, Margaret von Haubitz, who was abbess (head) of the convent, and her father's sister, Magdalena. In the nunnery, Katie spent her days praying and working obediently.

News of change in the church spread everywhere, even to the cloistered nuns in the convent at Grimma. In 1522, they heard that some of the monks had left the monastery for public life and were even marrying. They also learned of Martin Luther's teaching that salvation comes only by faith in Christ and not by anything a Christian can do on his own.

This was news indeed to the young nun who had been taught that she must *earn* forgiveness and her way to heaven.

Some of the nuns at Grimma agree with Luther's writings.

Katie and 11 others send a secret message to Luther ...

Dear Dr. Luther, We need your help! We beg you to ...

Luther contacts a merchant who sold goods to the convent.

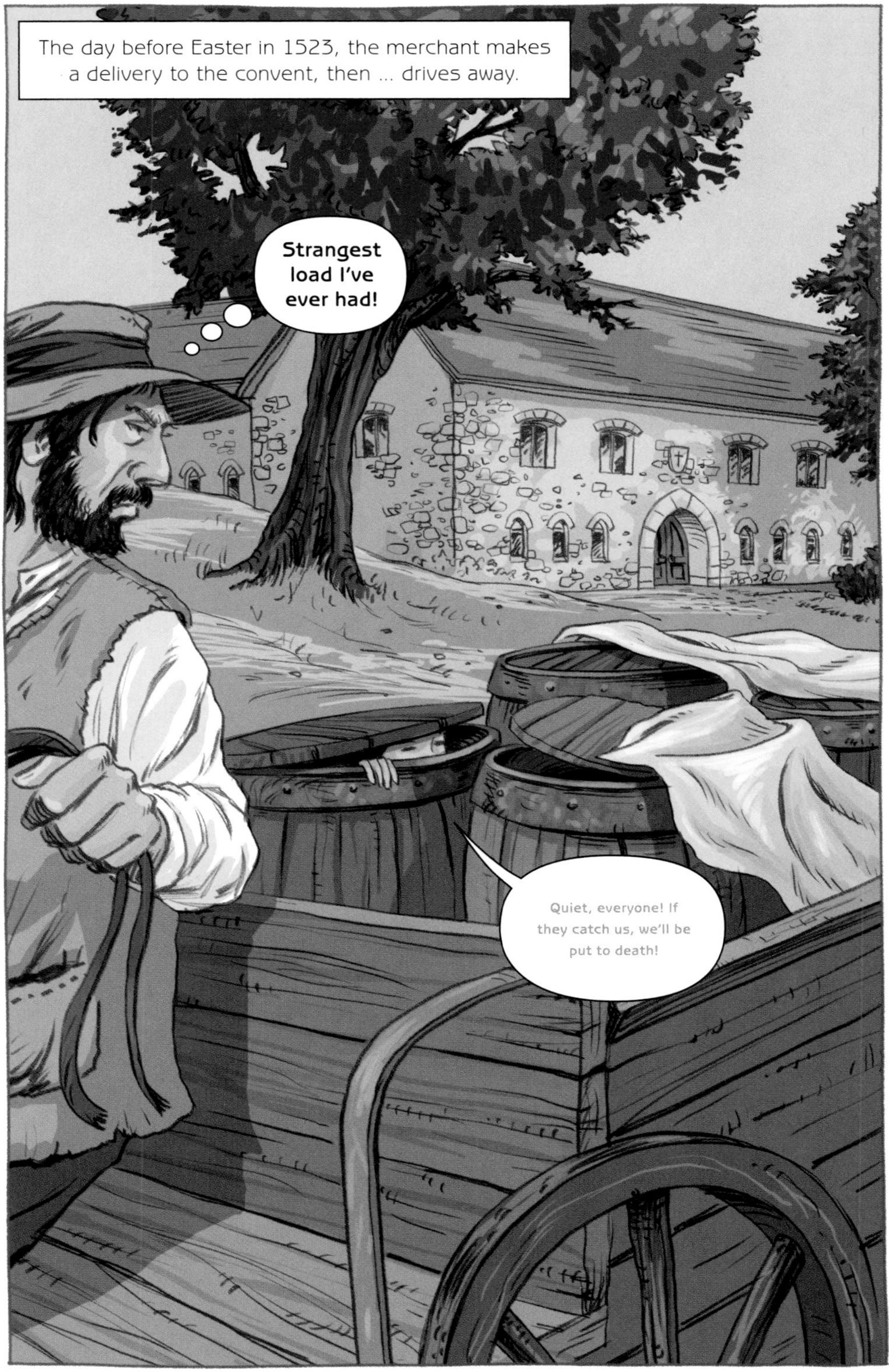
The day before Easter in 1523, the merchant makes a delivery to the convent, then ... drives away.
Strangest load I've ever had!
Quiet, everyone! If they catch us, we'll be put to death!

After their escape, the nuns bid one another farewell. Three of the women go home. The others go to Wittenberg, where they find work as governesses. Many them also find husbands.

Katie's story continues when she falls in love with Jerome Baumgaertner. But when he leaves Wittenberg and never returns, she is heartbroken.

Martin Luther has someone else in mind for her to marry, a Pastor Glatz. The strong-minded Katie does not agree.

Never! I will *not* marry *him!*

But she *does* get married!

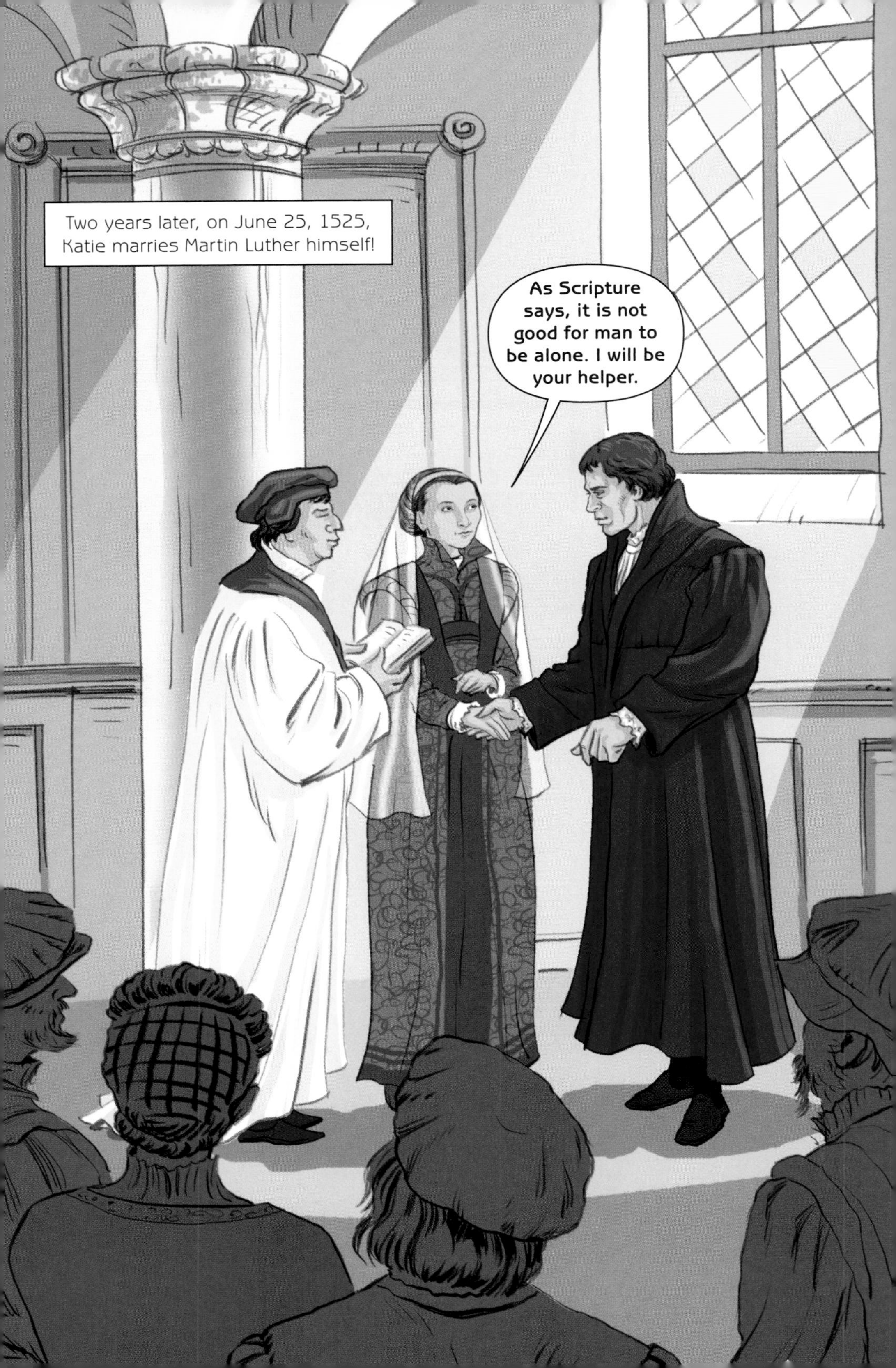
Two years later, on June 25, 1525, Katie marries Martin Luther himself!
As Scripture says, it is not good for man to be alone. I will be your helper.

The marriage suited them both. They shared mutual respect and devotion, as well as deep dedication to the work of the church. Katie was intelligent and strong, and was a great help to Martin in his daily life.

Life in the Luther home was happy.

When the Augustinian monastery in Wittenberg closed, Elector John the Steadfast gave it to the newlyweds. It was a large estate and Katie managed it well. She ran the farm, raised cattle and sheep, and ran a brewery—all to earn enough income to keep the household going and to provide Martin time to write, teach, and preach.

Martin was generous to everyone, often giving food and money to students. He also opened their home for travelers, students, and relatives, who might stay for weeks or even months. During these times, he hosted lively discussions with students and other theologians. Many of these discussions were recorded in his

Table Talks.

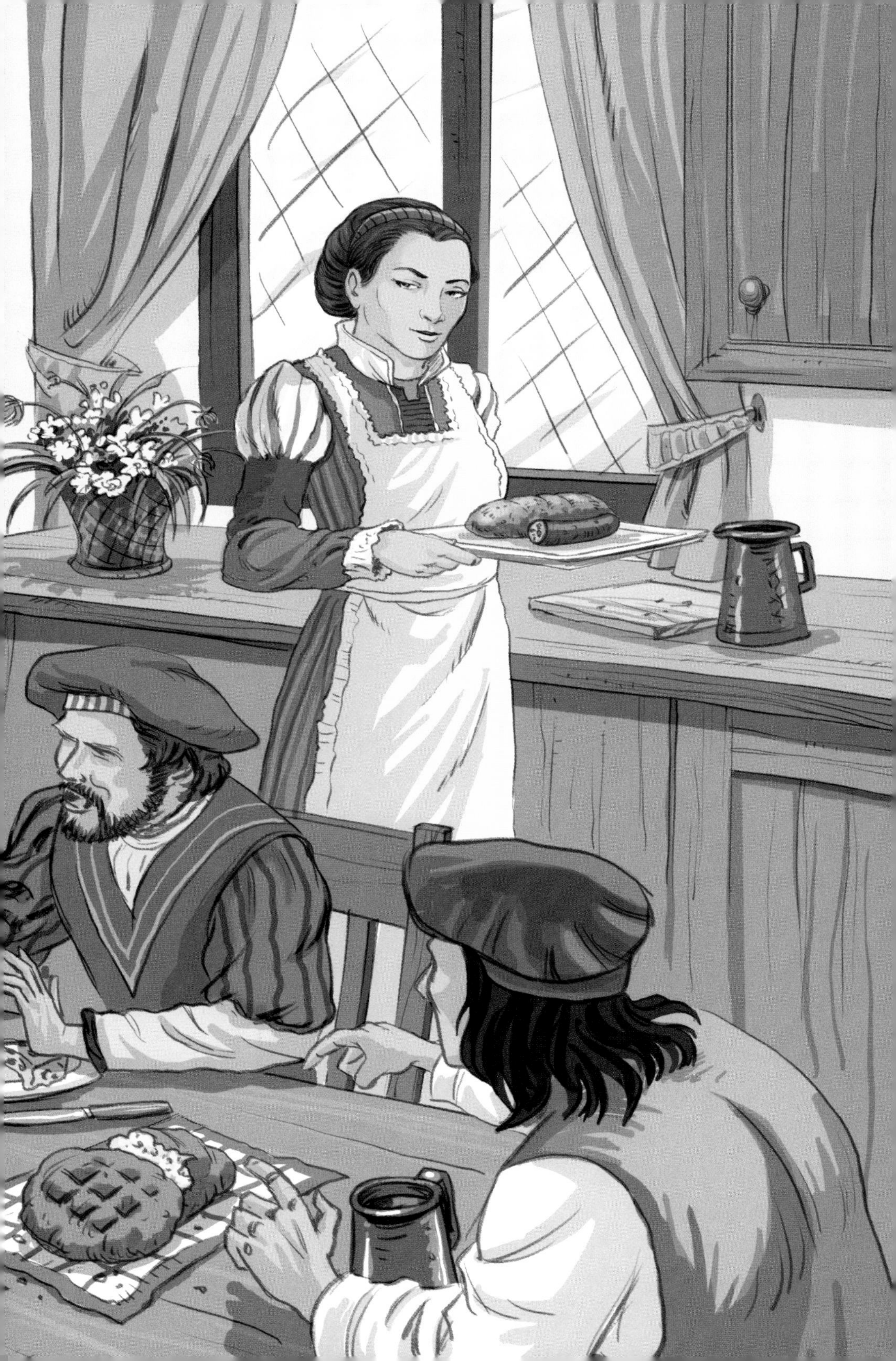

Martin and Katie are blessed with six children: Hans, Elizabeth, Magdalena, Martin Jr., Paul, and Margaret.

Luther is strict with their children, but he loves joining them as they play, and he often writes songs for them.

When he travels, he writes long, loving letters to Katie and their children.

Greetings and peace. My Lord Katie, I pray for your good health and I hope to return this week to you and our children ...

And Martin traveled often!

His work in the new Protestant Church body often took him away from home to settle disputes. Following Luther's example, others throughout Europe voiced their own beliefs. Many of these theologians agreed with Luther's teachings, but many did not. These men would gather at meetings and conferences to work out their disagreements. Luther attended many of these gatherings, and he published many books and pamphlets that explained the faith and that helped keep the church unified.

But hard work, stress, and illness took their toll on Martin Luther. His health was not good. He had chronic stomach and heart problems, and he sometimes became deeply depressed.

" Faith is a living, daring confidence in God's grace,

so sure and certain that a man could stake his life

on it a thousand times. "

❖ The Reformation Continues

In 1529, Charles was finally successful in ending the war between Spain and France. And once again, he turned his attention to the enduring problems in the church. For the first time in nearly 10 years, he returned to Germany. This time, Charles called the German Church leaders to the

Diet of Augsburg

to settle the arguments once and for all and to enforce the Edict of Worms. Charles wanted both sides to come together. So, he invited the Protestants to present their beliefs in writing, and he promised to give them a fair hearing. Martin Luther, Philip Melanchthon, and other Protestants responded to the emperor's invitation by writing a collection of documents that eventually became known as the **Augsburg Confession**.

But they were not the only ones who were writing their statement of beliefs. **John Eck**, a long-time Luther opponent, published a document called *404 Articles for the Diet in Augsburg*, which explained what he thought was wrong with Lutheran teachings—including some things that were not true.

▪ Who was Philip Melanchthon?

Born Philip Schwartzerdt in 1497 (he changed his name to Melanchthon, the Greek equivalent of his last name), Philip was a scholar, professor, theologian, and author. He studied many subjects, including philosophy, astronomy, law, and mathematics. He was a Greek scholar and a professor at the University of Wittenberg. Melanchthon and Luther met at that university and became good friends.

Melanchthon is considered a great reformer, second only to Martin Luther. He made many important contributions to the church, including the Augsburg Confession and the organization and explanation of Reformation beliefs. And he represented Luther at important meetings such as the Diet of Augsburg. He wrote many books about the Bible, about preaching, and about teaching. In addition to his work in the church, he reformed the entire education system in Germany, which became the standard for schools throughout all of Europe.

After Luther died, Melanchthon became a key leader of the Lutheran Church and continued to defend, guide, and shape it until his own death in 1560.

There is great excitement in Augsburg on June 15, 1530, when Charles arrives. Here is the emperor of the Holy Roman Empire—the most powerful man in the world! Charles is greeted by church bells, cannon blasts, and the shouts of thousands.

Come! Let us put an end to all disagreements!

But later that evening, after an elaborate church service, Charles orders the German Lutherans to stop preaching. When they refuse, Charles loses his temper.

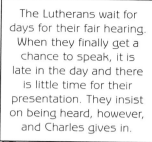

The Lutherans wait for days for their fair hearing. When they finally get a chance to speak, it is late in the day and there is little time for their presentation. They insist on being heard, however, and Charles gives in.

I will hear your case, but not until tomorrow afternoon.

The room where the hearing takes place can hold only 200 people. To make up for that, the Lutheran representative speaks loudly so that the people outside the room can hear too.

We are ready, God willing, to present more information according to the Scriptures.

Throughout the 1520s, Luther had been enjoying freedom in Germany, but the Edict of Worms was still in effect. He was still an outlaw. For his safety, he stayed behind at Coburg castle—a four-day carriage ride from Augsburg. He was bitterly disappointed, but he didn't waste time by moping. He spent those weeks in waiting by continuing with his writing. He had many visitors, too. But he was not part of the important events at the Diet. To add to his disappointment, Martin received very bad news. His father, Hans, had died.

The speech is effective. Some people who had supported the Roman Church finally understand the Lutheran cause.

I've been misinformed about what you Lutherans really teach.

It is the truth, the pure truth; we cannot deny it!

One of the German princes asks John Eck to prove that the Lutheran writings are wrong.

I can, indeed, prove the Lutheran writings wrong, if I use the writings of the Church Fathers. ... But not if I use the Scriptures.

Now Charles is not sure what to do. He seeks advice from the Catholic princes and professors. Then he asks Eck and the other Catholics to show where the Lutheran confession is wrong. They do; they give Charles a document that is more than 350 pages long!

Your hatred shows up on nearly every page. Do it over, and this time answer with the Bible.

It took Eck a month to rewrite, but when he finished, his response was only thirty-one pages long. This new document was filled with Bible passages, but it did not prove where Luther and his followers were wrong. What it did do was once more demand that the Lutherans abandon their teachings and accept those of the Roman Church.

Still, they refused.

Charles was in a very difficult spot. His goal was to reunite the church, but neither side would compromise. And he still needed the support of the German people— although the war between Spain and France was over, the threat from the Ottoman Empire was still very strong.

Charles was not ready to give up just yet. He appointed a committee of seven Catholics and seven Lutherans. They met and discussed and wrote, but they were no closer to agreement. While this committee was meeting, Philip Melanchthon wrote a defense of the Augsburg Confession and sent it to Charles.

Charles refused to read it. He insisted that the Lutherans rejoin the Roman Catholic Church and gave them a deadline: April 15, 1531. He also forbade them from publishing any new books about their beliefs or from trying to convert others to their side.

And the church was still divided.

▪ Ulrich Zwingli

As reform was sweeping the German Church, a similar movement swept throughout Switzerland. It was led by Ulrich Zwingli.

Zwingli's life story parallels Luther's in many ways. He was born in 1484, just two months after Luther. He studied for the priesthood, and when he was 22, Ulrich moved to Glarus, a small mountain town, to be the priest there. During his 10 years in Glarus, Zwingli studied the Bible. As he did, he began to question some of the church's practices that were not in agreement with God's Word.

After serving as chaplain to Swiss soldiers from Glarus, Zwingli became involved with politics. When he was 35, he was appointed chief pastor of the cathedral in Zurich, one of the nation's largest cities, and began making dramatic changes in both church practice and city government. He got married and had a family. Eventually, Zwingli's reform got him in trouble. He was banned from preaching, yet he continued to preach.

Zwingli and Luther were contemporaries in church history. They agreed on some things that reformed the church, but they did not agree on everything. One of the most significant disagreements they had was about the Lord's Supper. Luther proclaimed that Christ's body and blood are truly present in the Sacrament. Zwingli believed that the bread and wine were just symbols.

Like Luther, Zwingli put the Bible at the center of the Christian faith and taught that no other work is above it. He wrote hymns and published many books. Although his name is not as well-known, he is considered an important figure in the Reformation, though his teachings were often deeply wrong.

In the months after the Diet of Augsburg, both the emperor and the pope (now Clement VII) promised to invite the German Lutherans to a general council where they could continue to discuss their differences. The Lutherans doubted that they would be sincerely heard. The German princes did agree, however, that the many separate territories should pull together for mutual support.

And in the meantime, life in Germany went on. Martin continued to translate the Bible and to work with the professors at the University of Wittenberg. He and Katie grieved the loss of his mother, Margaret. And they endured.

So, what's a Lutheran anyway?

Today, we say that a Christian who *confesses* or believes, accepts, and lives by the teachings of Martin Luther is a Lutheran. But the first use of that word was by leaders of the Roman Catholic Church who were against everything Luther said and did. For Martin's part, he did not like the term. He wanted to be known simply as a Christian or as an evangelical. "What is Luther?" he said. "My teaching is not mine, nor have I been crucified for anyone."

The Bubonic Plague

Imagine living at a time and in a place where there were no antibiotics or other medications to treat disease. In the 1500s, people were terrified of illness, and for good reason! European cities were struck by the plague every few years. People died by the millions. Treatment was usually just guess-work and often was worse than the disease itself.

The Bubonic Plague, or Black Death as it was sometimes called, haunted Europe for centuries. It may have be spread by infected fleas. Victims usually died within a few days of infection. Other diseases were common too, including pneumonia and anthrax.

Even the Luther family was touched by this terrible disease. Baby Elizabeth died when she was only eight months old.

Does it surprise you that of all men, Martin Luther wanted reconciliation with the Roman Catholic Church? He did! Throughout his life, Luther yearned for the division in the church to be healed, and he claimed that all his writings and teachings were an effort to return the whole Christian Church to the simple Gospel truths as revealed by God in His Holy Word.

To help his fellow Germans prepare for the general council with the pope (now Paul III) and the emperor, Luther wrote the **Smalcald Articles**. This collection of writings defined Lutheran doctrine, and some people believe that it is

Luther's most important work.

This general council—called **The Council of Trent**—is one of the most important in the history of the Catholic Church. Beginning in 1545, it met many times throughout more than 20 years, but for many reasons, the Lutherans were not allowed to participate.

Now the dean of the theological school at Wittenberg, Luther lectures to students and publishes books on God's Word and about theological topics.

In 1539, Katie suffers a miscarriage. Martin spends as much time at his wife's bedside as he can.

Let us find peace in the One who cares for us better than the angels can.

His own health continues to worsen. Luther has been troubled by digestive problems since he was a young man. As he grows older, he develops heart problems, kidney stones, and arthritis. And he is often treated for infections in his throat and ear and for a sore on his leg.

There were still constant threats from enemies of the Protestant Church and of Germany. To remind his family and his congregation about God's promises, Luther wrote a hymn that he titled *A Hymn for the Children to Sing Against the Two Arch-enemies of Christ and His Holy Church—the Pope and the Turks*. Christians today know it well as a prayer to the triune God:

> *Lord, keep us steadfast in Your Word;*
> *Curb those who by deceit or sword*
> *Would wrest the kingdom from Your Son*
> *And bring to naught all He has done.*
>
> *Lord Jesus Christ, Your pow'r make known,*
> *For You are Lord of lords alone;*
> *Defend Your holy Church that we*
> *May sing Your praise eternally.*
>
> *O Comforter of priceless worth,*
> *Send peace and unity on earth;*
> *Support us in our final strife*
> *And lead us out of death to life.*

Luther needed such words of encouragement.

When his daughter Magdalena died at 13, he was deeply depressed. He saw perpetual disagreements among church members, devastation caused by the plague in Wittenberg, and his own failing health—so Martin Luther prepared for the end times.

Luther is often called on to settle arguments among his people. One such disagreement is between two brothers, Gebhard and Albert, counts of Mansfield.

Although he doesn't feel well, and the weather is bad, Luther travels the 80 miles to Eisleben to meet with them.

He stays in Eisleben for three weeks. While he is there, he preaches several times at the local church ...

... and he is successful in helping the men settle their argument.

But this trip takes a great toll on Martin Luther. He falls ill that very day.

I am not well. I have pain in my chest and must lie down to rest.

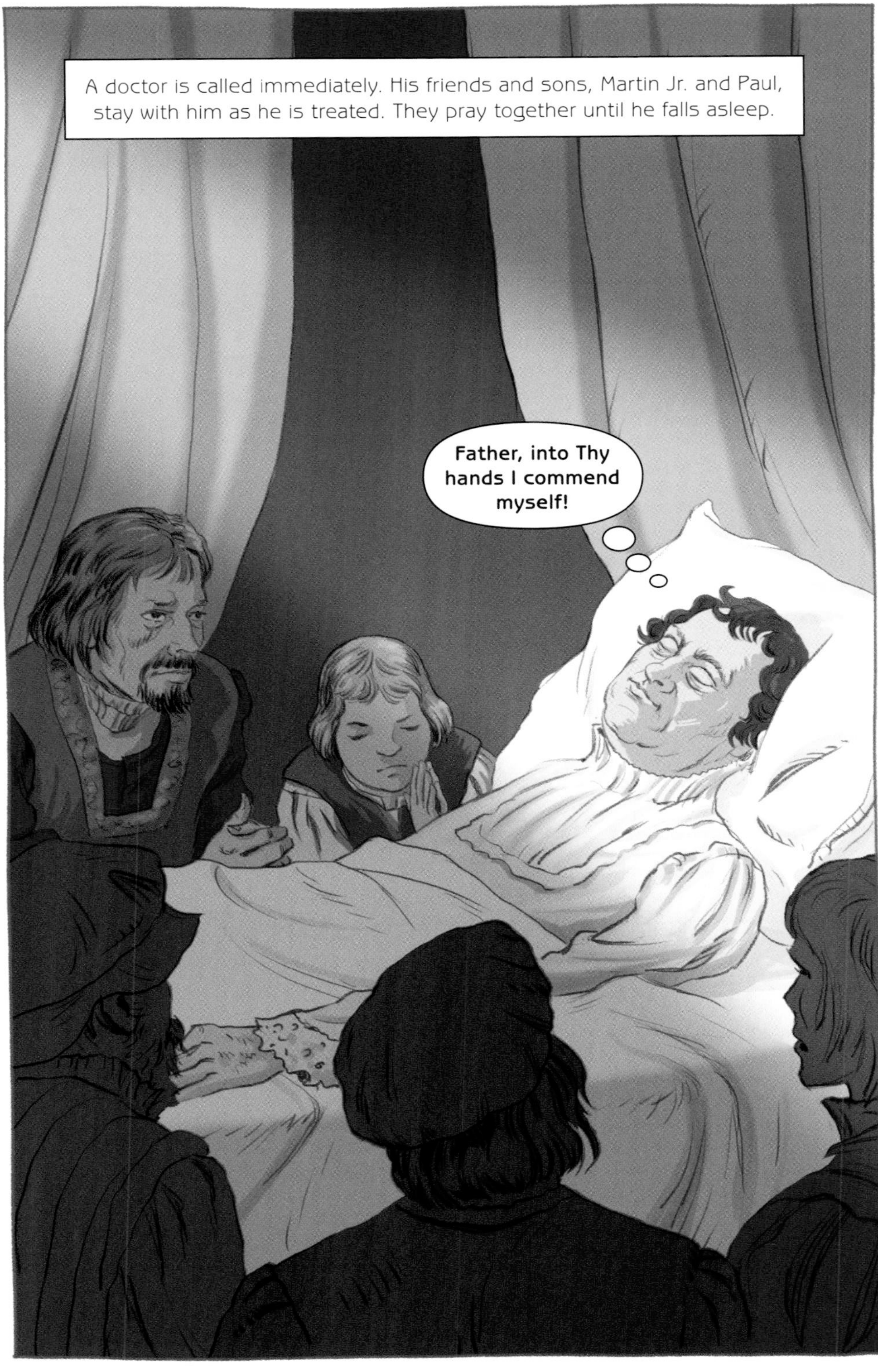
A doctor is called immediately. His friends and sons, Martin Jr. and Paul, stay with him as he is treated. They pray together until he falls asleep.
Father, into Thy hands I commend myself!

During the middle of the night, Martin Luther awoke. He was in great pain, caused by a heart attack. His friends tried to comfort him as best they could. And he prayed,

"I thank You that You gave Your dear Son, Jesus Christ, for me, in whom I believe, whom I have preached and confessed, loved and praised. . . ."

This was the last prayer he ever prayed.

Martin Luther died at about three o'clock in the morning on February 18, 1546.

Luther's funeral takes place the day after he died. It is held in St. Andrew's Church, where he delivered his last sermons.

As his coffin is carried back to Wittenberg, it is followed by a crowd of church leaders, politicians, students, and friends.

Luther's body is carried into Castle Church, through the door where he nailed the Ninety-five Theses ...

... and is buried in the floor before the pulpit where he preached.

HERE LIES THE BODY OF
MARTIN LUTHER,
DOCTOR OF SACRED THEOLOGY,
WHO DIED IN HIS HOMETOWN EISLEBEN
IN THE YEAR OF OUR LORD 1546
ON THE 18TH DAY OF FEBRUARY
AFTER HAVING LIVED FOR 63 YEARS,
2 MONTHS, AND 10 DAYS.

Word about Luther's death traveled throughout Germany and the rest of Europe. His enemies believed that the split in the church would soon be healed and the Roman Catholic Church would be reunited at last. But we know now that the opposite happened.

After his death, Luther's popularity increased. His books were distributed throughout all Europe, Britain, Asia, even Australia, and island nations. Men like Philip Melanchthon continued to preach and teach the Lutheran Confessions. And the Reformation grew.

And why is this? Why has

Martin Luther's legacy

continued to influence the Christian Church and scholarship from the 1500s until this very day?

It is because he never wavered from the truth.

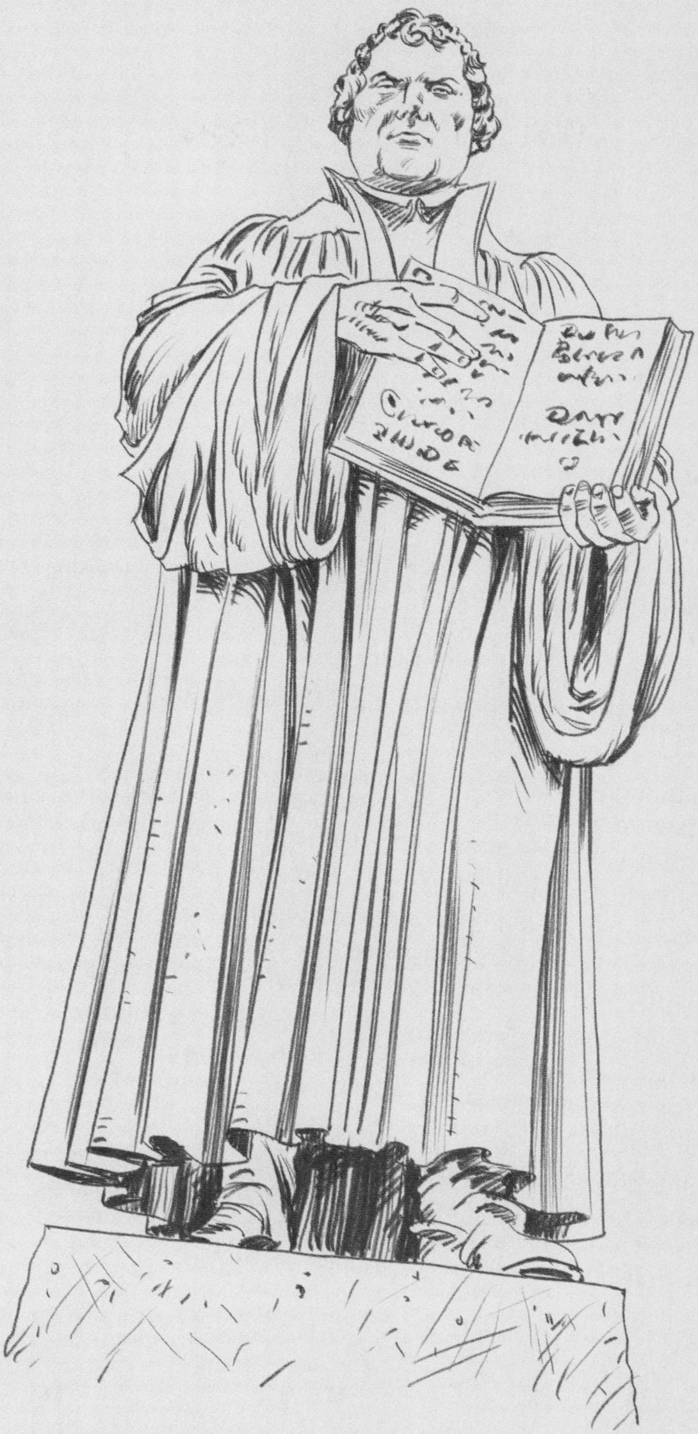

▪ Luther's Seal

Martin Luther designed this seal while he was a university professor at Wittenberg. His explanation goes like this:

The first thing expressed in my seal is a cross, black, within the red heart, to put me in mind that faith in Christ crucified saves us.

"For with the heart man believes unto righteousness."

- Now, although the cross is black, shameful, and intended to cause pain, yet it does not change the color of the heart, does not destroy nature. In other words, it does not kill but keeps alive. "For the just shall live by faith"—by faith in the Savior.

- But this heart is fixed on the center of a white rose to show that faith causes joy, comfort, and peace. The rose is white, not red, because white is the ideal color of all angels and blessed spirits.

- This rose, moreover, is fixed in a sky-colored background, to show that such joy of faith in the spirit is but a promise and beginning of heavenly joy to come. This joy, though not yet revealed, is looked forward to and held by hope which we have.

- Around this background is a ring, to show that such bliss in heaven is endless. And since the ring is made of gold, the best and most precious metal, it also shows that the bliss of heaven is more precious than all other joys and treasures.

If you would like to learn more about Martin Luther, we suggest *Luther: Biography of a Reformer* by Frederick Nohl, published in 2003 by CPH. The creators of this graphic novel drew heavily from that source text, which tells the story of the Reformation in greater detail and includes beautiful full-color stills from the movie *Luther*.

You might also be interested in learning more about the church Luther inspired. Following is a short list of books that will help.

These books were written by Martin Luther for the purpose of teaching the basics of the Christian faith:

Luther's Small Catechism with Explanation (Concordia Publishing House, 2005)

Timeless Bible Truths: The Illustrated Small Catechism (Concordia Publishing House, 2010—this is the content of the Small Catechism told in a marvelous visual style.)

Luther's Large Catechism with Study Questions (Concordia Publishing House, 2010)

These books are about the Lutheran faith:

Lutheranism 101 (Concordia Publishing House, 2010)

The Spirituality of the Cross: The Way of the First Evangelicals (Concordia Publishing House, 2008)

The Lutheran Study Bible (Concordia Publishing House, 2009)

Concordia: The Lutheran Confessions (Concordia Publishing House, 2007)

If we were to use one word to describe what was happening in the world during the 1500s, it would be change.

New technologies and unprecedented courage sparked exploration and invention, art and literature, ideas and philosophies. The Reformation caused great and permanent change in the church. The Ottoman Empire commanded vast areas of Europe, Asia, and the Mediterranean and caused great anxiety for Charles of Spain, the world's most powerful man. The Ming Dynasty was at its height in China. England saw the rise and fall of Henry VIII and the beginning of the Elizabethan era. And Spain and Portugal explored, conquered, and claimed most of the New World.

1450

Florence is the center of the Renaissance. The Incas rule Peru. Ottoman Turks have conquered Constantinople. Johann Gutenberg invents movable type and opens a print shop in Mainz, Germany. This invention is key to the Renaissance and the Reformation, and is said by some to be the most significant invention of the millennium.

1455 Gutenberg prints his first Bible.

1462 Ivan the Great rules Russia.

1480 The Spanish Inquisition begins. Ferdinand Magellan is born in Portugal.

1482 Portuguese explorers discover bananas on the coast of Africa.

1483 **Martin Luther is born in Eisleben, Germany.**
England's Richard III is crowned king.

1484 Ulrich Zwingli, who will bring the Reformation to Switzerland, is born.

1485 Leonardo da Vinci studies flight and illustrates models of mechanical wings, which inspire the modern-day helicopter. The War of the Roses ends when King Richard III is killed in battle.

1492 Columbus becomes the first European to encounter the Caribbean.

1497 Vasco de Gama sails around Africa and discovers the sea route to India. John Cabot reaches Canada and discovers Newfoundland.

1498 Da Vinci paints *The Last Supper*. Vasco de Gama reaches India.

1500 Portuguese navigator Pedro Alvares Cabral discovers Brazil.

1501 Louis XII conquers Italy.

1502 Michelango begins work on *David*. Frederick the Wise founds the University of Wittenberg.

1503	Leonardo da Vinci paints the *Mona Lisa*. Nostradamus is born.
1504	Columbus brings cocoa beans from the New World to Spain. Chocolate drinks become a Spanish favorite.
1505	**Martin Luther enters a monastery.**
1506	The building of St. Peter's Church, Rome, is started. Christopher Columbus dies.
1507	The first recorded epidemic of smallpox in the New World (Hispaniola). Pope Julius II begins selling indulgences to fund construction of St. Peter's Church.
1508	Michelangelo begins painting the ceiling of the Sistine Chapel.
1509	Henry VIII is crowned king of England. Peter Heinlein invents the watch.
1510	**Luther represents his monastery in Rome.** England is struck by the "great plague." The first black slaves arrive in the Americas (Santo Domingo, Haiti).
1512	Ponce de Leon claims Florida for Spain. Copernicus proposes that the sun is the center of the solar system.
1513	Balboa crosses the Isthmus of Panama and becomes the first European to sail on the Pacific. Portuguese explorer Jorge Alvares arrives in China. Pope Julius II dies and Leo X is named pope.
1514	Pope Leo allows the sale of indulgences to continue to fund the building of St. Peter's Church.
1515	Portugal establishes a trade route to India.
1516	Charles becomes king of Spain.
1517	**Luther posts his Ninety-five Theses.** Sebastian Cabot discovers Hudson Bay.

1519	Ulrich Zwingli begins reformation in Switzerland. Hernando Cortes conquers Mexico for Spain, brings horses to America. Charles of Spain is chosen Holy Roman Emperor. Magellan sets out to circumnavigate the globe, using five ships given him by Charles of Spain. Leonardo da Vinci dies.
1520	Suleiman becomes Sultan of Turkey. Montezuma dies.
1521	**Luther is excommunicated.** Magellan is killed in the Philippines. The Ottomans conquer Belgrade.
1524	Magellan's expedition completes its voyage around the world. Verrazano, sailing under the French flag, explores the New England coast. The Peasants' War in southern Germany begins.
1525	Frederick the Wise dies and John the Steadfast becomes Elector.
1526	Babur gains control over India.
1527	Pope Clement VII is imprisoned and the Italian Renaissance ends. The Protestant Reformation begins in Sweden.
1529	**Luther publishes the Large Catechism and the Small Catechism.**
1530	**The Augsburg Confession is presented to Charles V.**
1531	Smalcaldic League is formed. The Inca civil war is fought.
1532	Pizarro conquers the Incas in Peru. Ottomans invade Hungary. John the Steadfast dies; his son, John Frederick the Magnanimous, becomes elector.
1533	Henry VIII is excommunicated. Three-year-old Ivan the Terrible becomes czar of Russia.

1534	**Luther publishes his complete translation of the Bible.** Jacques Cartier claims Quebec for France. The Ottomans capture Baghdad.
1535	Henry VIII marries Anne Boleyn and makes himself the head of the English Church. Sir Thomas More is executed. Jacques Cartier sails up the St. Lawrence River and Canada is claimed for France.
1536	Henry VIII has his wife Anne Boleyn executed so he can marry Jane Seymour. John Calvin establishes Protestantism in Switzerland.
1539	Hernando de Soto explores inland North America. The first printing press is set up in North America (Mexico).
1540	First known Native American composition is written. Thomas Cromwell is executed.
1541	John Knox leads the Reformation in Scotland and establishes the Presbyterian Church there. Henry VIII becomes king of Ireland. The Amazon is discovered by Francisco de Orellana.
1542	Hernado de Soto explores the Mississippi River. Portuguese traders land in Japan.
1543	Nicolaus Copernicus publishes his theory that the earth revolves around the sun. The first illustrated study of the human body takes place. Portugal begins trading with Japan.
1545	Council of Trent begins.
1546	**Martin Luther dies at Eisleben on February 18.**
1548	Firearms are used for the first time in a battle in Japan. The Ming Dynasty closes all ports in China to foreign trade.
1549	The Book of Common Prayer is published in England.
1550	Mongols invade China and besiege Beijing.
1552	Katie Luther dies, December 20.

1553	Mary I restores Roman Catholicism in England.
1554	Portuguese missionaries establish Sao Paulo in Brazil.
1556	The first music book is printed in the New World. The Shaanxi Earthquake (history's deadliest) strikes China.
1558	Queen Elizabeth I ascends the throne in England and restores Protestantism in England. Shakespeare, Marlowe, and Spenser help the Elizabethan era reach its height.
1561	Persecution of Huguenots in France ends, for a time, before the French religious wars begin again.
1563	Council of Trent ends, establishing the Roman Catholic Church.
1564	Michelangelo dies.
1568	Mary, Queen of Scots, flees to England..
1570	Ports in Japan open to foreign ships. Queen Elizabeth I is excommunicated by Pope Pius.
1580	Francis Drake returns to England after circumnavigating the globe. The Book of Concord is published in Germany.
1582	The Gregorian calendar is implemented.
1584	William of Orange is assassinated. Sir Walter Raleigh founds the Roanoke Colony in Virginia.
1587	Mary, Queen of Scots, is executed. The first Catholic mission is established in America (St. Augustine, Florida). Virginia Dare is the first European child born in the Americas.
1588	The Spanish Armada is defeated.
1590	The dome of St. Peter's basilica is completed. Galileo describes the theory of gravity.

SUSAN K. LEIGH is an editor and author who lives in a small town in Illinois. She began her career in publishing as a contributing writer for her high school yearbook, worked as a newspaper reporter during college, and then as a magazine editor for a dozen years. After a three-year-stint as an advertising copywriter, she began a day job as a book editor and has stayed put.

Susan is the author of several children's picture books, including twelve titles in the "God, I Need to Talk to You" series.

When she isn't writing, Susan is knitting, gardening, or playing with her grandtwins, Jack and Kendall.

DAVE HILL graduated from Glasgow School of Art in 1983 and began his career as a painter with exhibitions in Glasgow, Edinburgh, Liverpool, and London.

He then worked in the video game industry for ten years as a concept artist producing character and environment designs in both 2D and 3D.

As a freelance illustrator, Dave's passion is children's books, although he has also illustrated comic books, storyboards, greeting cards, and product packaging.

Dave produces most of his work digitally although he still dabbles in traditional media, painting in oils and watercolor.

He lives in Scotland with his wife, Anne, and their two children, David and Amy.

www.davehillsart.co.uk